Responses to 101 Questions
on Catholic Social Teaching

Responses to 101 Questions on Catholic Social Teaching

Kenneth R. Himes, O.F.M.

PAULIST PRESS
New York/Mahwah, N.J.

Cover design by Jim Brisson

Library of Congress Cataloging-in-Publication Data

Himes, Kenneth R., 1950–
    Responses to 101 questions on Catholic social teaching by Kenneth R. Himes.
        p. cm.
    Includes bibliographical references.
    ISBN 0-8091-4042-X (alk. paper)
    1. Sociology, Christian (Catholic)—Miscellanea. 2. Catholic Church—Doctrines—Miscellanea. I. Title: Responses to one hundred and one questions on Catholic social teaching. II. Title. III. Series.

BX1753 .H54 2001
261.8′088′22—dc21

                                                                                        2001035160

Published by Paulist Press
997 Macarthur Boulevard
Mahwah, New Jersey 07430

www.paulistpress.com

Printed and bound in the
United States of America

CONTENTS

LIST OF QUESTIONS ON CATHOLIC
   SOCIAL TEACHING   vii

PREFACE   1

ONE: GENERAL BACKGROUND   3

TWO: ECCLESIOLOGICAL ISSUES   13

THREE: FOUNDATIONAL THEMES   23

   A. *COMMUNITARIANISM*
   B. *HUMAN DIGNITY*
   C. *HUMAN RIGHTS*
   D. *COMMON GOOD*
   E. *JUSTICE*
   F. *SOCIAL LIFE*

FOUR: POLITICAL LIFE   51

FIVE: ECONOMIC LIFE   61

SIX: INTERNATIONAL LIFE   81

SEVEN: SPECIFIC CONCERNS   101

BIBLIOGRAPHY   113

LIST OF QUESTIONS ON
CATHOLIC SOCIAL TEACHING

One: General Background

1. What is meant by Catholic social teaching?
2. Some people say that Catholic social teaching is "the church's best kept secret." Why?
3. Where do you find this social teaching?
4. What are these documents and where can I find them?
5. Do all the writings of CST come out of Rome?
6. Is liberation theology another way of talking about the social teaching of the church?
7. Since the tradition of CST has developed over time, are there stages in the development of the teaching?
8. Who writes these documents, the pope and the bishops?

Two: Ecclesiological Issues

9. Since the literature of the CST has been written by popes, groups of bishops, individual bishops and various advisors then I have to ask, what authority does this teaching have?
10. It would seem from your remarks that some statements or even parts of statements have more authority than others. So am I a so-called bad Catholic if I disagree with my bishop about a political or economic issue?
11. What is the role of the conference of bishops in this country in regard to CST?

12. We are talking a lot about the pope and bishops, but what role is there for lay people in the formulation of CST?

13. Are there any examples of lay social action involvement around now?

14. Why does the church get caught up in political and economic issues that others should be dealing with instead of doing the one thing the church is supposed to do, serve the spiritual dimension of life?

15. Even if I accept that the church should be involved in public life, or perhaps can't help but be involved, that does not settle how it should be involved in a nation that believes in the separation of church and state. What about the first amendment?

16. I'm confused. Are you saying there are no legal limits on the church's role in politics, that priests can tell me whom to vote for in their homilies?

17. Does CST ever address issues of justice within the church itself?

Three: Foundational Themes

A. Communitarianism

18. Is there a basic perspective or idea that runs through the documents of CST?

19. This emphasis on the communal aspect of being human is appealing but can you say more about it?

20. You mentioned individualist and collectivist errors. What are you talking about?

21. Perhaps I am asking this question because I am an American, but what about personal freedom? It does not seem from what I know that the Catholic Church has always struck the right balance between the individual and the community.

B. Human Dignity

22. Why is human dignity the starting point for the teaching?

23. Doesn't starting with human dignity feed the American emphasis on the individual instead of the community? Maybe we should stress the communitarian approach instead.

24. I can think of people who behave so badly, they act in such an inhumane way, that they sink below the level of human dignity. Can people lose their dignity?

25. What is the connection between human rights and human dignity?

C. Human Rights

26. What are the human rights that the church endorses today?

27. That's a pretty long list of rights. How does the church decide something is or is not a human right?

28. Are you suggesting that as social conditions change a person's human rights change?

29. Why have human rights become so important to CST?

D. Common Good

30. Can you explain what is meant by the common good?

31. When I hear language like "serve the common good" I begin to worry about personal freedom. Some talk about the common good sounds an awful lot like socialism. Isn't the common good a socialist idea?

32. But who defines what is the common good?

33. What do you mean by solidarity?

34. What is meant by the "preferential option for the poor"?

E. Justice

35. What does the church mean by justice?

36. Can you say more about "participation" as an approach to justice?

37. You said that the biblical meaning of justice is different than the usual way the word is understood by Americans. What do you mean?

38. There seem to be several kinds of justice mentioned in the documents. Can you explain them?

39. You have not mentioned social justice in your comments. Where does the church use the term in its teaching?

40. Could you say more about social justice and how it relates to the other forms of justice?

41. When I was educated in the Catholic school system I used to hear a lot more about the virtue of charity than justice. What is the relationship of charity to justice?

F. Social Life

42. How is the family envisioned in CST?
43. As someone who works as an economist, it seems to me that part of what explains CST's emphasis on social justice is that the teaching has been formulated in a period when the social sciences have given us new insights into our world. What do you think?
44. We need personal conversion because each of us is a sinner. If we need to have social conversion, does that mean society is a sinner?
45. I am a little confused. I have heard of original sin and actual sin that is mortal or venial. Where did this social sin idea come from?

Four: Political Life

46. Among the key social institutions is the state. What is the role of the state according to CST?
47. Charging the state with protecting and promoting the common good makes for a pretty expansive description of the state's role in social life, doesn't it?
48. What are those norms governing the state's role?
49. Can we summarize subsidiarity to mean that "smaller is better" or "the less government the better"?
50. I understand what you have been saying, but the impression I have is that church teaching endorses a large role for the state in economic affairs. Is that not so?
51. What, then, does the church say about big government programs such as food stamps or public housing?
52. What do you mean that the pope's communitarianism influences his view of the welfare state?
53. With all this talk about participation, I conclude that CST is a strong defender of political democracy as the best form of government. Am I correct?

Five: Economic Life

54. What occasioned Leo XIII's writing on the economic situation?
55. If it is the plight of workers that CST first addressed, how does the tradition understand the experience of work?
56. I have read that John Paul II did manual labor before he became a priest. Does he have any particular views on human work?
57. I'm not sure I understand this idea of "co-creation." Can you say a little more about it?
58. How does the church view labor unions?
59. You mentioned there have been criticisms of labor unions in CST. What are they?
60. Among the basic rights of labor which CST has proposed is that of a just wage. What is meant by a just wage?
61. What exactly is the view of the church regarding poverty?
62. A lot of attention with talk of a just wage and the care of the poor seems to be about a floor below which people should not fall, but does CST talk about a ceiling above which people should not rise?
63. I'd like to get a bit more specific. How much of one's goods ought to be donated in charity?
64. Is the church's teaching on capitalism one of approval or disapproval?
65. If capitalism gets a conditional approval, what are the conditions?
66. What about the papal view of private property? Is it critical or approving?
67. Has the teaching on private property evolved over the years?
68. Considering Leo's opposition to socialism, does the church distinguish between socialism and communism?
69. One of the most important institutions in modern capitalism is the corporation. What do we find about corporations in CST?
70. Is there anything in CST on the phenomenon of multinational or transnational corporations?
71. I'm a "white-collar" worker who doesn't own the company where I am employed. Does the church have anything to say directly to individuals who work in corporations as managers?
72. I think it is fair to say that CST was formulated in an age of industrial labor and agricultural work. What can CST say to people

employed in a postindustrial economy, whether we call it an "information society" or a "service economy"?

73. Not everyone works at computer stations or in marketing, sales and research labs. Some folks are still working the land. Is there any teaching about farm life and agriculture?

Six: International Life

74. In a number of your responses you have touched on matters that go beyond the nation-state. Are there any documents that focus specifically on the international context of social issues?

75. If Jesus is our true peace and if we will only know that peace in our hearts, why should bishops or any of us focus on political ideas about peace rather than the spiritual?

76. What does CST mean by the just war tradition?

77. What are the criteria that CST lists for a just war?

78. A concern I have is how we can stand by and watch innocent people suffer at the hands of dictators who are little more than thugs. What does CST say about the possibility of humanitarian interventions?

79. Frankly, I don't understand how we can talk about a just war. Maybe in the past this was possible, but today it simply is impossible to see the destruction caused by modern weapons and believe there is anything just about it. When will the church give up on the just war tradition and simply say "war is wrong, period"?

80. Don't you think we should talk less about just war and more about peace?

81. Can you explain where pacifism fits into CST?

82. You said that the bishops at Vatican II endorsed the right of Catholics to refuse to participate in war. Do you mean conscientious objection?

83. What does the church say about the arms race?

84. Speaking of great evils, I heard someone say the Catholic Church teaches that the gap between rich and poor nations is the great evil of our time. Is that true?

85. What is the remedy for the gap between rich and poor?

86. What is "integral development"?

87. So is just and integral development the basic message of CST on this topic?

88. Is any other dimension of development needed to grasp the approach of CST?

89. One issue that received a lot of attention during the Holy Year 2000 is the jubilee theme of debt forgiveness. Does CST address the issue of international debt?

90. A key role in debt relief and numerous other questions in international life is played by global institutions such as the World Bank, the International Monetary Fund (I.M.F.) and, of course, the United Nations. What has CST to say about these organizations?

91. Obviously, a major global issue today is the health and integrity of our environment. What does CST say about the concerns of the ecological movement?

Seven: Specific Concerns

92. What does CST have to say about women in society?

93. Does CST say anything about racism and race relations?

94. A big issue in my region of the nation is immigration. What, if anything, does CST have to say about immigration?

95. It seems as if the death penalty has become a concern in this country and I know that John Paul II opposes it. What does CST say about capital punishment?

96. In all your comments, I get no sense that CST has an ecumenical aspect. Does ecumenism figure in the tradition of CST?

97. I don't mean this in a mean-spirited way, but can you say that CST made any difference in the real world of American politics, economics and culture?

98. Since my primary experience of the church is what happens in my parish, what can we do at the parish level to advance CST?

99. Is there much attention given to spirituality in CST?

100. I'd like to put you on the spot for two questions. First, up until now you have done your best to put a good face on CST. What criticisms of CST do you think are legitimate?

101. My final question also asks you to take a risk. Can you predict the future of CST?

To Michael

For the pleasure and privilege of being your brother

PREFACE

For more than two decades I have lectured on, written about and taught Catholic social teaching. It is more than a professional academic interest, however, since I believe there is a wisdom resident in the tradition that can aid in healing and transforming our societies and our world. Often after speaking at a religious education conference or a parish gathering I have found people eager to ask questions, intrigued by the topic of Catholic social teaching. They were seeking to know more than could be conveyed in a brief (or not so brief!) lecture.

When my former colleague Lawrence Boadt, C.S.P., now the publisher/president of Paulist Press, asked me to write this book, I realized it gave me a chance to revisit some of the more frequently asked questions. To make sure the questions I had been asked were indeed the sort of questions that people have, I called on friends for assistance. Patricia Lamoureux of St. Mary's Seminary in Baltimore, John Carr, Joan Rosenhauer, Rich Fowler and Gerry Powers of the U.S. Catholic Conference and Leslie Griffin of Santa Clara University all gave me their lists of common questions. There was a remarkable amount of convergence in the lists, so I trust that I have gotten the questions right. As for the answers…well, I best leave that to the reader to decide.

Translating the oral give-and-take of a question-and-answer session into written prose inevitably forces some changes. A certain informality and colloquial way of speaking gets lost. What is gained is that I have been able to insert certain relevant citations into my answers, citations that I am unable to quote with exactness when standing at a podium without notes.

My hope is that readers will follow the citations to look at the documents themselves. Admittedly, much of the writing in the documents cited makes them no threat to dislodge Harry Potter from the best-seller list. But not everything that is good for us has to be pleasurable, or so my parents told me.

The customary closing caveat for an author is to say that much more could be said about the topic but that space prevents it. I will avail myself of the usual caution. There are limits to this kind of format for a book and some questions that others have had are not the ones I have about the tradition.

In any event, I do not presume this little volume substitutes for reading the documents of our social tradition nor do I claim that it will satisfy those with more scholarly interests in Catholic social teaching. I will be happy if what I provide serves to introduce an important part of the Catholic tradition to some of my fellow pilgrims on the journey.

ONE

GENERAL BACKGROUND

1. What is meant by Catholic social teaching?

There is a broad and a narrow understanding to the expression *Catholic social teaching*. Viewed one way, Catholic social teaching (hereafter CST) encompasses all the ideas and theories that have developed over the entire history of the church on matters of social life. More commonly, as the term has come to be understood, CST refers to a limited body of literature written in the modern era that is a response of papal and episcopal teachers to the various political, economic and social issues of our time. Even this more narrow understanding, however, is not neatly defined.

No official list of documents exists; it is more a matter of general consensus which documents fall into the category of CST. Some documents (for example *Rerum Novarum,* an encyclical letter by Leo XIII) are on everyone's list while the Christmas radio addresses of Pius XII are cited by some but not all as part of the heritage. Most people, when referring to CST, use Leo's 1891 encyclical as a benchmark for the beginning of the tradition of social teaching. Yet not only did Leo write important encyclicals on politics before *Rerum Novarum* but a number of his predecessors promulgated significant statements on a variety of social matters. Thus, it can be argued that since the modern papal practice of issuing encyclicals began with Benedict XIV (1740–58) many of these pre-Leonine letters should be considered part of CST. (Michael Schuck's book *That They Be One* is a fine overview of the entire body of social teaching found in the papal encyclicals.)

Clearly, the expression CST is elastic, sometimes designating an expansive body of material and at other times used in a more constricted sense to identify a limited number of papal and episcopal writings dating from the papacy of Leo XIII. Perhaps we can understand the term *Catholic social teaching* as an effort by the pastoral teachers of the church to articulate what the broader social tradition means in the era of modern economics, politics and culture.

2. Some people say that Catholic social teaching is "the church's best kept secret." Why?

That is a statement I have often heard but I think the situation is changing. A good deal more attention is being given to CST now than in the past. The reason for the statement was the perception that this body of teaching was not given the emphasis in preaching, education and practice that other aspects of our heritage received. I believe that perception to be true, although, as I noted, it is changing. Before Vatican II, in many of the seminaries where our clergy were trained scant attention was given to the church's social teaching. Moral theology tended to focus on personal morality since clergy were being trained for hearing confessions. Many of us grew up in parishes where it would have been unusual to hear a sermon based on the social teachings of the papacy.

No generation of believers has ignored the moral implications of being a disciple. In every age Christians have tried to understand and follow the moral imperatives that flow from our baptismal commitment. At the same time, it must be admitted that the faith community has not always given equal weight to the entire breadth of the moral life. American Catholics who grew up in the middle decades of the twentieth century experienced a church that gave great emphasis to personal responsibility in the areas of religious duties, sexuality, family life and truth-telling.

While not simply ignored, it is fair to say that social topics such as economic justice, race relations, social welfare policy or human rights received considerably less attention in the common presentations of the Catholic understanding of the moral life. It is due to such a situation that the "best kept secret" statement was leveled as a charge against our failing to make known the riches of our church's teaching on social morality.

3. Where do you find this social teaching?

I have always liked the suggestion of the well-known priest-sociologist Andrew Greeley that there are low and high traditions of CST. The high tradition refers to the material contained in the official documents issued by those popes and bishops who serve the teaching office of the church. This high tradition is derived from a vision of human life in community—a series of metaphors, images and stories that reside in the imagination of people who have been profoundly shaped by their Catholic heritage. This imaginative vision is the low tradition of CST. In other words, the social teaching that we read in a papal encyclical is an outgrowth of a distinct way of viewing the world, which is characteristic of people who are marked by the theology and spirituality of Catholicism. So in the sense of the low tradition we can say that CST can be found in the religious imagination of men and women who have been shaped by the Catholic heritage.

Using Greeley's distinction, we can say that the high tradition of CST is the explicitly formulated theories of economic, political and social life that are expressed in papal, conciliar and other episcopal documents, and these documents draw from the social vision of the Catholic imagination.

4. What are these documents and where can I find them?

These documents are readily available in a number of translations and anthologies that can be purchased from bookstores or borrowed from a good library. I have already explained that there is no single list of these documents with which everyone agrees. In my own teaching I have settled on a roster of readings for students that is limited yet reasonably comprehensive. While other documents can justifiably be added I would say that a basic list is comprised by the following:

1891 Leo XIII	*Rerum Novarum* (On the Condition of Labor)
1931 Pius XI	*Quadragesimo Anno* (Reconstructing the Social Order)
1961 John XXIII	*Mater et Magistra* (Christianity and Social Progress)
1963 John XXIII	*Pacem in Terris* (Peace on Earth)
1965 Vatican II	*Gaudium et Spes* (Pastoral Constitution on the Church in the Modern World)
1965 Vatican II	*Dignitatis Humanae* (Decree on Religious Liberty)
1967 Paul VI	*Populorum Progressio* (On the Development of Peoples)
1971 Paul VI	*Octogesima Adveniens* (Call to Action)

1971 Synod	*Justitia in Mundo* (Justice in the World)
1981 John Paul II	*Laborem Exercens* (On Human Work)
1987 John Paul II	*Sollicitudo Rei Socialis* (On Social Concern)
1991 John Paul II	*Centesimus Annus* (One Hundred Years of Catholic Social Teaching)

If additions were to be made to this list for the sake of understanding the historical development of CST then I would suggest: *Diuturnum, Immortale Dei* and *Graves de Communi* by Leo XIII, all of which dealt with aspects of church-state relations and an understanding of democratic regimes; *Divini Redemptoris* by Pius XI on socialism; the Christmas radio addresses of Pius XII reflecting on international affairs; *Evangelii Nuntiandi* issued by Paul VI, which, among other matters, reflected on the relationship between the social mission of the church and its religious identity; John Paul II's first encyclical, *Redemptor Hominis,* which presented the anthropological and Christological foundations for his social teaching, and his encyclical *Evangelium Vitae,* addressing life-issues and public policy, as well as the papal speeches given before the United Nations.

5. Do all the writings of CST come out of Rome?

All the documents listed above are examples of teaching that was meant to be universal, that is, the intended audience was the entire church or even all humankind. In addition, there have been a number of very important statements issued by episcopal conferences or individual bishops addressed to their local situations. Notable in this regard are the pastoral letters of the U.S. bishops, *The Challenge of Peace* and *Economic Justice for All.* They have also issued numerous statements addressing such issues as the environment, racism, immigration, capital punishment, abortion and public policy. A good way to acquaint yourself with the U.S. bishops' social teaching is by reading their statement *Faithful Citizenship: Civic Responsibility for a New Millennium,* which offers a summary listing of the many issues on which the bishops have articulated a moral position.

The documents issued by the Latin American bishops during their conferences at Medellin, Colombia, and Puebla, Mexico, also merit attention and study. As might be expected, the amount of literature produced by the various bishops' conferences is quite extensive, but not all is of the same quality or of the same interest to readers from regions beyond the intended audience. Nor are many of these documents easily accessible to people without access to a good research library. Yet these episcopal documents should be considered as contributions to CST. (A very useful survey of many episcopal documents has been written by Terence McGoldrick, "Episcopal Conferences Worldwide on Catholic Social Teaching" in *Theological Studies,* vol. 59 [1998], pp. 22–50.)

6. Is liberation theology another way of talking about the social teaching of the church?

Liberation theology has multiple dimensions. It might be best to talk about liberation theologies. Feminist theology can be understood as a form of liberation theology as can African-American theology as well as other theological movements in and beyond Catholicism. Many of the theologies that share a family identity as being liberation theologies take up questions of economic, political and social life. But it would be a mistake to reduce the agenda of liberation theologies to the topics traditionally examined in CST. For instance, Latin American liberation theologians have long been insistent that they are examining the whole range of theological subdisciplines in their work: Christology, ecclesiology, sacramentology, spirituality, biblical studies, fundamental moral, trinitarian theology. They understand themselves to be employing a method of reflection not focusing on a set of topics within a branch of theology. Clearly, something similar can be said of feminist theology.

Nevertheless, many recent theological movements have sought to promote social change that would benefit a given group directly and, by extension, the entire church and humankind. In that sense it may be the case that a large part of the energy and direction of various liberation theologies is akin to the concerns of CST. As John Paul II has written: "To those who are searching today for a new and authentic theory and praxis of liberation, the church offers not only her social doctrine and, in general, her teaching about the human person redeemed in Christ, but also her concrete commitment and material assistance in the struggle against marginalization and suffering" (*Centesimus Annus,* #26).

Additionally, it should be acknowledged that liberationist themes have entered into CST in the areas of international economics, social advancement, the connection between the social mission of the church and its religious mission, and especially the preferential option for the poor.

7. Since the tradition of CST has developed over time, are there stages in the development of the teaching?

This is a matter of opinion since there are various ways of identifying stages within the tradition. A simple way is to see each of the papacies as constituting a stage. Or, perhaps, we can simply divide the tradition into pre- and post-Vatican II materials. For myself, a more helpful approach is to look at the tradition of CST in terms of the focus of concern one finds in the writings. Viewed this way, I think it is possible to identify five overlapping stages with the principal documents for each stage.

- 1891—the plight of the working class in the domestic economies of the industrial age *(Rerum Novarum, Quadragesimo Anno, Mater et Magistra)*
- 1941—the need to establish a just and peaceful international political order (Pius XII Christmas radio addresses, *Pacem in Terris)*
- 1965—the role of the church in social life *(Gaudium et Spes, Dignitatis Humanae, Evangelii Nuntiandi)*
- 1968—building a just global economic order *(Progressio Populorum, Octogesima Adveniens, Justitia in Mundo, Sollicitudo Rei Socialis)*
- 1981—the meaning of economic life in the face of the two great ideologies of socialism and capitalism *(Laborem Exercens, Centesimus Annus)*

While by no means the only way to classify the evolution of the tradition, the above scheme is plausible. Other themes, of course, can be found in the documents and there are subthemes aplenty, but the focal issues listed above are a fair description of what dominates the stages, which merge into one another. The list should not be interpreted to mean that later popes were unconcerned about the working class or topics such as war and peace. What occurred with each stage was a shift in the framework of analysis, not the abandonment of previous concerns.

8. Who writes these documents, the pope and the bishops?

The only fair answer to the question is yes and no. Some popes have engaged the process of formulating an encyclical quite intensely, others have directed the process through commentary and editorial reaction but left the actual writing to others, and still others have delegated the task to trusted aides or scholars and signed off on the final version. John Paul II has been closely involved in the encyclicals he has promulgated that concern CST. As a philosopher and politically astute leader, he has a strong interest in the social mission of the church. His hand is evident in each of the documents mentioned above, but he does rely on the input and written formulations of a number of aides.

Many episcopal documents are the product of a collegial process typically involving a committee of bishops who discuss the issue and oversee the writing. Staff and consultants to the bishops draft proposed texts, and the members of the entire episcopal conference offer amendments and vote final approval of the document.

Therefore, one can conclude that the official documents of CST are indeed accurate expressions of the social views of the pastoral leaders of the church. At the same time, it is also accurate to say that many of these documents were worked on and written by a variety of people. It would be difficult to parse each document and determine who influenced what in the text. But the end result is a body of materials that the authoritative teachers within the church have approved, signed and promulgated as theirs.

Two

Ecclesiological Issues

9. Since the literature of CST has been written by popes, groups of bishops, individual bishops and various advisors then I have to ask, what authority does this teaching have?

Perhaps the first thing to be clear about is the nature of the authority of any church teaching. As believers, you and I are called to faithful discipleship, a commitment to live our lives as best we can by following the Lord Jesus. It is the word of God to which we pledge our lives. It is God's revelation in the history of Israel and particularly in the life and death of one Jew, Jesus of Nazareth, that is the foundation of our faith. When the pope or bishops teach, they are trying their best to interpret and understand the meaning of that revelation. So any teaching, be it an encyclical or speech or pastoral letter, should not be isolated from the broader tradition of our faith. If it is a good and wise teaching it will help us to understand God's word better.

Many Catholics concentrate on the *who* question: Did the pope teach this, or a group of bishops or one bishop? Prior to that, however, is the *what* question: What is being taught? When a high school religion instructor teaches the Catholic belief in the dignity of all people before God that teacher is stating a truth central to our faith. That this teacher is not a professional theologian, a bishop or pope does not make the teaching any less true or any less a claim that deserves our adherence. On the flip side, if the pope proposes a specific plan for resolving some economic hardship, such as the foreign debt of poor nations, the authority of the statement is hardly absolute since this is a matter several degrees removed from the explicit revelation of God's word. All this is to say that there are degrees of teaching in the church just as there are different levels of authority among those who teach.

10. It would seem from your remarks that some statements or even parts of statements have more authority than others. So am I a so-called bad Catholic if I disagree with my bishop about a political or economic issue?

Again, the topic cannot be answered with a simple yes or no. It is not just the person teaching that matters; it is also what is being taught. In the documents we are talking about, those that form the body of CST, you will find teaching from those who are charged with the responsibility of being the official pastoral teachers of the church, but you will find within these documents all different sorts of teaching. Some of the teaching is close to the heart of the gospel and other materials represent informed, sensitive, prudent judgments but not core beliefs of the Catholic faith.

Much of CST entails judgments involving a complex process of bringing moral values into dialogue with a variety of historical and empirical elements. The competence of the church to teach is always rooted in its fidelity to God's revelation. When CST states a moral principle, such as the duty to care for the poor, it is difficult to see how a person could challenge the teaching and not be losing touch with the gospel. But when a document of CST offers a judgment about whether this or that economic policy provides a marginally better advantage for the poor we are dealing with another kind of teaching.

A good example of distinguishing between different levels of teaching can be found in the American bishops' pastoral letter on war and peace. One finds there the explicit declaration "that not every statement in this letter has the same moral authority. At times we [the bishops] reassert universally binding moral principles....At other times we reaffirm statements of recent popes and the teaching of Vatican II. Again, at other times we apply principles to specific cases" (*The Challenge of Peace,* #10). Now it would be nice if all the documents of CST made these distinctions clear and even identified which claims fit into which category, but that is not the case. So we need to be careful readers to avoid claiming either too much or too little authority for a given teaching.

11. What is the role of the conference of bishops in this country in regard to CST?

While national or regional conferences of bishops have issued documents on a number of questions, it is precisely in the area of CST that many have been most active. Here in the United States, the National Conference of Catholic Bishops (NCCB) has certainly made social teaching a key area of its work. And there is nothing surprising about this when we consider the nature of social teaching. Because of the great variety of socioeconomic and political arrangements around the world it is not easy to formulate a social message that is equally pertinent or applicable to every nation. Thus, many bishops have thought it quite natural for themselves as teachers to examine the situation within their own countries in the light of CST. Paul VI in his letter commemorating the eightieth anniversary of *Rerum Novarum* encouraged this attitude when he wrote that local churches should "analyze with objectivity the situation which is proper to their own country..." (*Octogesima Adveniens,* #4).

The NCCB has been particularly far-sighted in this respect. They have made provision for solid staffing by qualified professionals to assist them in the area of CST, and invested a good deal of time and energy as an episcopal body in advancing the social mission of the church by addressing the concrete circumstances of American life. As a result, many of the pastoral letters of the U.S. bishops have been widely hailed as substantial contributions to the body of literature that makes up CST.

12. We are talking a lot about the pope and bishops, but what role is there for lay people in the formulation of CST?

Let me answer in two steps. First, there is the abundant evidence that many lay people have shaped the thinking of the papacy on social issues. Leo XIII was a man of patrician roots who was familiar with the intellectual movements that engaged Catholics of his social class. In the latter part of the nineteenth century, a variety of such movements studied the situation of the working class and reflected upon the role for people of faith, both as individuals and as a church, in resolving social problems. A network of "social Catholics" representing a broad range of viewpoints examined the issues through conferences, publications, letter writing and discussion groups. Leo breathed the air found in this atmosphere and drew upon many of the ideas, both in his analysis and his recommendations, when he composed *Rerum Novarum.* Similar, if not identical, sorts of influences can be attributed to a long list of lay scholars, writers, journalists, public officials and social activists in later papacies. The major documents of CST are not properly understood as the work of one person but are a result of much input, direct and indirect, from lay persons of various competencies. This is certainly the case with the major pastoral letters of the American bishops.

A second aspect of lay involvement in the formulation of CST is the invaluable work of numerous lay movements that have striven to implement the insights of CST. Putting the words into action has brought about deeper understanding and a better grasp of that which is truly wise in the teaching, what corrections are needed, and what adaptations must be made if the tradition is to foster the goal of building societies that allow people to live in dignity. In telling the story of CST we ought not overlook how the experience of the grass roots has often bubbled up through the church to become a new locus for reflection and the formulation of social teaching.

13. Are there any examples of lay social action involvement around now?

Certainly, just about anywhere you look you can find dedicated lay Catholics making a difference in their homes, neighborhoods, professions, work sites. In addition, numerous groups draw upon CST for inspiration and guidance as they take up the work of social justice. Some of them, still active today, date back to movements preceding Leo XIII, such as the St. Vincent DePaul Society started by Frederic Ozanam. Others grew out of the forces unleashed by Leo's teaching. The Catholic Worker movement instigated by Dorothy Day and Peter Maurin is an example. There are a variety of organizations, predominantly lay, that embody the values of CST. Some are explicitly connected to the church—Pax Christi, Catholic Rural Life Conference, parish credit unions, diocesan legislative networks—and some are not. But any number of groups exist that reflect Vatican II's teaching on lay engagement in the social mission of the church.

According to *Gaudium et Spes* it is important for lay men and women to "take on their own distinctive role." Christians "in the exercise of all their earthly activities" can gather together "their humane, domestic, professional, social and technical enterprises into one vital synthesis with religious values." This is properly the role of the lay person, to see that the values of the gospel are "inscribed in the life of the earthly city" (#43).

In a recent statement of the American bishops the point is well made that it is not a matter of people working in explicitly identified and sponsored church groups. Rather, individuals and groups can enflesh CST in the faithful performance of their roles as parents, workers, citizens, consumers and similar daily activities. The bishops note that "Catholics are everywhere in this society. We are corporate executives and migrant farm workers, politicians and welfare recipients, educators and day care workers, tradesmen and farmers, office and factory workers, union leaders and small business owners." As a result it is possible for "Catholics to be instruments of God's grace and creative power in business and politics, factories and offices, in homes and schools, and in all the events of daily life" *(Everyday Christianity: to Hunger and Thirst for Justice).*

14. Why does the church get caught up in political and economic issues that others should be dealing with instead of doing the one thing the church is supposed to do, serve the spiritual dimension of life?

It may seem at times that the church is meddling in affairs it should leave alone. And I will not defend the details of every statement the church has made about public life. But your question goes beyond specific disagreements and questions CST in principle.

One of the contributions of Vatican II to CST was to place the social mission on firm theological foundations. You can find the position in *Gaudium et Spes.* The basic framework of the argument made by the bishops moves in four steps:

1. The council fathers state that the church "is at once a sign and a safeguard of the transcendence of the human person" (#76). This commitment to human dignity has religious significance since it is rooted in a religious claim about the mystery of creation. The biblical account of Genesis tells us that each human being is made in God's image.

2. At the same time we must be able to fulfill this charge of being "a sign and a safeguard" without the church becoming simply another humanitarian organization or one more social welfare agency. Our mission is not political but religious, to be of service to the reign of God.

3. By emphasizing the religious mission of the church there is no attempt to dismiss the importance of earthly life. The power of God's reign must reach out to transform all aspects of human existence; it must not be reduced to some otherworldly realm apart from our temporal lives.

4. Therefore, political, social and economic consequences will flow from pursuit of the church's religious mission. The bishops cite four areas where the religious mission spills over into social concerns: commitment to the defense of human dignity, promotion of human rights, fostering unity among members of the human family, and discerning the deeper significance of human work and activity (see *Gaudium et Spes,* #40–43).

In sum, while the church must transcend every political system because of its religious mission it must still engage the social order due to the implications its religious mission has for temporal life.

15. Even if I accept that the church should be involved in public life, or perhaps can't help but be involved, that does not settle how it should be involved in a nation that believes in the separation of church and state. What about the first amendment?

You are absolutely right. The question of why the church is involved is distinct from how the church should be involved. If you understand that the church's social mission is a consequence of its religious mission, that means certain activities which are legitimate for other nonreligious institutions may not be so for the church. So there are self-imposed limits that the church should accept in order to avoid its religious mission becoming overwhelmed by political or economic goals, for example, endorsing a political party or movement as the Catholic party or movement.

But what you state suggests there may be limitations that are not self-imposed but rather required by the first amendment of the U.S. Constitution. We must remember that the constitutional separation of church and state means that organized religion will receive neither favor nor obstruction from the state. What is unconstitutional is state establishment of religion or prohibition of the free exercise of religion. The amendment prohibits what the state can do in respect to any church. Nothing in the first amendment should be interpreted as separating the churches from society nor religion and morality from public life. On all matters in the public forum, organized religion is free to speak and act. Whether the religious voice gets heard is another matter and will depend on the persuasiveness of its message.

16. I'm confused. Are you saying there are no legal limits on the church's role in politics, that priests can tell me whom to vote for in their homilies?

What I am saying is that the limits on the church's activity are not so much a matter of law as a matter of social custom and, more importantly, a matter of good theology. If a priest stands in a pulpit and tries to dictate to a congregation how it should vote, he may jeopardize the tax-exempt status of the parish but he breaks no law. The real standards he violates are those of good theology and common sense. Good theology suggests that the preaching role for the church's ministers is to help people understand their lives through the lens of the gospel and grasp the implications of the gospel message for daily life. When a church official makes concrete political judgments about a politician or a specific policy proposal, however, there is far more at work than simply the gospel. A host of judgments about economic contingencies, political consequences, historical circumstances and the like are involved when we make prudential judgments about particular candidates and their platforms. Common sense dictates that we make such judgments with a measure of modesty since we are far removed from the clarity and certainty we may have about a general moral principle.

We ought not underestimate the complexity that ordinarily is involved in moving from moral principles to political choices. Nor should we confuse the gospel's message with an individual's understanding of how that message might be interpreted for a highly contingent and fluid situation. Homilists and teachers can and should challenge a community to examine the values at stake, to search out the available options, to bring one's faith to bear on our choices in social life. But that is something different than advocating a partisan position when acting in one's official capacity as a religious leader.

17. Does CST ever address issues of justice within the church itself?

Yes, but admittedly not as candidly or comprehensively as many might like. I am omitting the recent discussions of the church's admission of guilt for certain sins and John Paul II's papal apology in preparation for the new millennium. Rather, I focus on the documents of CST and here the key statement is that of the bishops assembled at the 1971 synod. They were forthright in stating that "everyone who ventures to speak to people about justice must first be just in their eyes" (*Justitia in Mundo,* ch. 3).

From that fundamental acknowledgment the bishops went on to state that the church must respect the rights of all including women and laymen, opening up access to power and means of participation in the church's life. The bishops also called for respect for freedom of expression and fair judicial procedures.

On the matter of the church's wealth the synod statement announced the principle that "our faith demands of us a certain sparingness in use, and the Church is obliged to live and administer its own goods in such a way that the Gospel is proclaimed to the poor" *(Ibid.).* This led to a call for an "examination of conscience" on the matter of lifestyle including that of the bishops themselves as well as all church members.

Within the pastoral letter on the economy written by the U.S. bishops there is a serious attempt to discuss the role of the church as an economic actor. Crucial to that discussion is the statement that *"all the moral principles that govern the just operation of any economic endeavor apply to the Church and its agencies and institutions; indeed the Church should be exemplary"* (*Economic Justice for All,* #347, emphasis in original). The bishops then proceed to comment upon a variety of issues where the church is an employer: wages and salaries, employee rights, investments and property.

One finds in CST not apologies or condemnations regarding church failures but exhortations to do better. Those exhortations are, of course, implicit admissions that the church itself has not always acted in a just manner.

THREE

FOUNDATIONAL THEMES

A. *Communitarianism*

18. Is there a basic perspective or idea that runs through the documents of CST?

Remember when I discussed how the church explains its social mission (Q. 14) that I quoted the bishops at Vatican II who said the church "is at once a sign and a safeguard of the transcendence of the human person" (*Gaudium et Spes,* #76)? It can be said that the human person is the fundamental concern of social teaching. But it is a certain understanding of the person that CST presents. Perhaps one could say that understanding is marked by the two fundamental claims of human dignity and human sociality.

Certainly, human dignity is a recurring theme in the documents. So much else that is said flows from the foundational claim about the dignity of the person made in the image of God. But we must appreciate that the God in whose image we are made is Trinitarian. That is, we believe within the very nature of God there is an eternal celebration of loving communion.

A corollary to the claim that human beings are creatures made in the image of a Trinitarian God is that people are created for love. We exist for the purpose of entering into the experience of loving communion. Human beings are not meant to live in isolation but are meant to live in community with each other. We find ourselves precisely in the act of giving ourselves away to another and receiving the gift of another into our lives. Sociality is a key hallmark of the Catholic view of the human: "for by our innermost nature the person is a social being" (*Gaudium et Spes,* #12). This understanding of the person lends itself to a view of community as natural and necessary if persons are to achieve their full stature. Or, in the words of the American bishops, *"Human dignity can be realized and protected only in community"* (*Economic Justice for All,* #28).

19. This emphasis on the communal aspect of being human is appealing but can you say more about it?

The perspective of CST accentuates the personal responsibilities, organizational structures and cultural institutions that are necessary for community life to prosper. This perspective for viewing social questions provides a certain inflection when the church speaks of human dignity. It has been called a *communitarian* outlook. This term is employed to designate a family of social theories that focus on the conditions and institutions necessary for the experience of community.

There is a tendency in our minds to equate community with rather intense, intimate personal relationships. But I am not presuming a political or economic order that follows an extended family model of human relations. Rather, the term *communitarian,* when applied to CST, may be understood as an approach that promotes certain emphases in political, economic and social theory.

Politically, a communitarian theory emphasizes the import of the common good and the responsibilities of various participants, including the state, to promote the common good. Social contract theories highlighting individual liberties and rights will have a different emphasis. A scheme of international politics dominated by the ambitions of nation-states will likewise reflect a vision of global order different than one that promotes an international common good.

Economically, a communitarian approach will place the accent on mutual ties of interdependence that require cultivation of solidarity across class lines and between nations. As a result, the communitarian vision finds fault with unregulated free market approaches that permit significant inequalities or overlook the marginalization of persons from economic activity.

In the area of social theory, communitarianism prizes those networks of human association that are not so much chosen but into which we are inserted. Within the communitarian tradition human fulfillment is attained not simply in the achievement of autonomy but in acknowledging mutuality. Thus, attention is given to sociality as well as rationality when describing the human person with an accompanying concern for family, neighborhood, ethnic and religious roots as integral parts of human experience.

Placing CST within the communitarian school helps to explain the tendency in Catholic teaching to react negatively to the errors of both individualism and collectivism.

20. You mentioned individualist and collectivist errors. What are you talking about?

If one looks at the papal literature, especially the earlier documents, there is evident opposition to what is judged to be the twin evils of modern society, liberalism and socialism. This may cause confusion unless we realize that today in the United States we use these terms differently than in CST.

Liberalism in CST is actually closer to what many in this nation think of as conservatism or, more accurately, libertarianism. That is, liberalism in its earliest formulations championed free market capitalism, minimal state activity in public life and personal liberty in cultural matters. It was a theory that valued individual freedom above other goods. CST identified such a social theory as being individualistic in the extreme.

Socialism according to CST can be seen as an overreaction to liberalism. Socialists opposed laissez-faire capitalism and encouraged state intervention, even control, of the economy. Personal liberties were to be overridden in the name of the good of society. And, even more troubling, socialism was viewed as antithetical to religion due to its materialism. As well, family and other social groups could be overwhelmed since it was collectivist in the way it related the individual to the state.

Thus, liberalism and socialism, as they were defined in CST, became the incarnation of individualism and collectivism, respectively. Liberalism and socialism have evolved a great deal over time, of course, as has CST. But the authors of CST have generally understood the Catholic vantage point as more attentive to issues of community than liberalism allows while not ignoring the values of personal freedom as it charges socialism does. So one might see CST as a tradition that tries to strike a balance between two faulty extremes. In doing so it has developed affinities with other communitarian approaches.

21. Perhaps I am asking this question because I am an American, but what about personal freedom? It does not seem from what I know that the Catholic Church has always struck the right balance between the individual and the community.

Your question could be answered in a variety of ways. One way of addressing your concern is to acknowledge that CST did not emerge full-blown as a coherent and comprehensive social theory. It is important to remember that the major documents which give voice to the tradition are very frequently documents written in reaction to something. So one can read CST as occasional teaching that arises out of dialogue with the social conditions of the age.

As such, the tradition of teaching has evolved and one of the engines of change has been the dialogue between liberalism and Catholicism. Liberalism may have its flaws, but it also has its virtues and as these became apparent the church began to integrate the insights of the liberal tradition into CST. Appreciation for democratic politics, rights of conscience, limited constitutional state powers, separation of church-state, the linkage of human dignity with personal freedom and individual rights—these are all areas where CST has been refined through interaction with liberal experiments in a variety of nations.

If one sees the protection and promotion of human dignity as being the starting point for CST, it is possible to see how ever deeper investigation into the meaning, elements and implications of human dignity has led CST to borrow, interpret and build upon liberalism's insights as well as challenge its errors. (*Catholicism and Liberalism,* ed. by R. B. Douglass and D. Hollenbach is a scholarly collection of essays that examines many sides of the encounter between Catholicism and liberalism.)

B. Human Dignity

22. Why is human dignity the starting point for the teaching?

That human dignity is the point of departure for CST should be no surprise to people who confess two beliefs, that humans are made in the image of God and that the God who is creator of all entered into history through the Son and became human. In other words, the doctrines of creation and incarnation, central affirmations of our creed, lead us to affirm the dignity of each person.

Human beings are creatures of dignity and worth not because of any achievement on our part. Nor is our dignity traced to society's conferral of it. Our dignity is founded upon a faith-conviction, the doctrine of the *imago Dei*. We are creatures made in the image of the Creator.

This claim is further underscored when we consider the mystery of the incarnation. To state that when God wanted to be something other than God then God became human, says something not only about God but about the human. What Jesus of Nazareth reveals is that there is something about the human which makes us open to receiving God. That the finite is capable of receiving the Infinite is a wondrous claim about the person.

It is this faith-informed reading of the mystery of the human person that is the starting point of CST. The church does not take up social issues because it is driven by some partisan agenda but as a result of the theological claim that human beings are creatures of dignity and worth. If that claim is not to be reduced to pious sentimentality, then it must lead its adherents to work for the promotion of people's dignity and protection from whatever threatens that dignity.

The "unpacking" of the implications of the above paragraph is the story of the historical development of CST.

23. Doesn't starting with human dignity feed the American emphasis on the individual instead of the community? Maybe we should stress the communitarian approach instead.

I appreciate the sentiment behind your question, but there is a fundamental misconception that we must be clear about if we are to understand CST. The misconception is to read human dignity in an individualistic manner. When the Catholic tradition speaks of human dignity, it understands that the realization of dignity will always be in the context of community. There are a variety of ways this can be demonstrated but let me suggest one approach.

If you look at the two stories of creation found in the book of Genesis you see the teaching that human beings are essentially social. In the second account of creation God states: "It is not good for the human being to be alone" (Gen 2:18). There is the insistence that the person is meant to be in relationship, and so the reason humans are created as male and female is precisely so that they be driven to seek each other. Humanity is meant for companionship.

In the earlier creation account of the first chapter we read: "And so God created the human being in God's image; in the divine image did God create the human being, male and female did God create them" (Gen 1:27). Now the point is not that to be in the divine image means to have gender. God is neither male nor female; God is relational. For the Hebrew writer God is the God who creates in order to enter into covenant with the creature. God is relational and to be in the image and likeness of such a God means that humanity is meant to be in relationship. We are our true selves when we are in relationship, not as isolated beings.

Therefore, when CST affirms the dignity of the person this is not a reading of the person as an isolated individual. Rather, the communitarian emphasis of CST situates human dignity within a dense web of relationships. Human beings are most fully alive, most truly in touch with the dignity of their nature, when they are able to acknowledge the profound links existing between themselves and God, other persons and the rest of creation.

24. I can think of people who behave so badly, they act in such an inhumane way, that they sink below the level of human dignity. Can people lose their dignity?

Two kinds of arguments come to mind when thinking this way. On the one hand, we can deny that some persons actually share in our human nature and, thus, it is no offense to their dignity to treat them in a manner one ordinarily would not employ when dealing with people, for example, slavery, torture, genocide. This is, of course, not the sort of argument CST could ever accept even if throughout history some believers have denied the full humanity of their victims.

On the other hand, one might accept the humanity of another but argue that if people act contrary to their nature they surrender their dignity. For instance, if the emphasis is that human beings are essentially rational, it could be argued that if we act irrationally we act contrary to our nature and thereby we lose our dignity.

The question is, can we forfeit our dignity? Can we alienate, that is surrender, our dignity? CST says "no" since our human dignity is inherent and is neither conferred by society or state nor dependent on any achievement or claim we make for it. Therefore, it is not ours to surrender nor can others take it away. Our dignity is rooted in God's affirmation of our being.

This does not settle all questions surrounding such acts as punishment or killing, but CST clearly holds that even punishment and killing must be done in such a way that the dignity of the person is not violated. So we may never treat others in a manner that violates or rejects their human dignity. In our time, we have commonly expressed this conviction about the nonforfeiture of human dignity by talking about human rights that are inalienable and fundamental.

25. What is the connection between human rights and human dignity?

Human rights give shape and substance to the idea of human dignity. There is a danger that talk of human dignity remains merely a catchphrase devoid of any substance. In order to avoid that eventuality CST has articulated, over the years, a list of rights that spell out the conditions which secure and protect human dignity.

By the nature of the relationship between dignity and rights, the foundation for any legitimate human right is the dignity of the person while respect for the human rights of a person gives moral content to the idea of human dignity. Without their foundation in human dignity the language of human rights would be open to the charge that they are arbitrary claims made by individuals pursuing whatever good they wish. Rights-talk needs to be grounded by appeal to a value or norm that has broad consensual support. At the same time, by specifying what is meant by human rights we promote those moral claims that give content to human dignity and prevent it from becoming a vague notion to which all can pledge allegiance while doing whatever they please. So the connection is reciprocal.

Because CST bases its theory of human rights on human dignity it offers an approach that is distinctive from what is found in liberalism or socialism. Liberalism's focus on freedom has led to great emphasis on the importance of civil and political liberties. Socialism's concern for equality has inspired claims for social and economic goods. CST's reliance upon human dignity permits an analysis of the person that identifies a set of needs, freedoms and relationships which give content to human dignity (John Paul II, 1979 *U.N. Address,* #13).

This more inclusive approach means that CST endorses many of the liberties which liberalism champions while also affirming certain socioeconomic goods promoted by socialism that address needs essential for human dignity. And CST's communitarian perspective refuses to ignore those vital relationships of family, ethnic group, church community and the like that are important to support for human welfare.

C. Human Rights

26. What are the human rights that the church endorses today?

It was John XXIII who provided the first attempt at a list of human rights endorsed by the church (*Pacem in Terris,* #11–27). The 1971 Synod of Bishops proposed a right to development (*Justitia in Mundo,* chap. 1), and John Paul II has written of a right to a safe environment (*The Ecological Crisis: A Common Responsibility* [1990 World Day of Peace Message], #9) and to economic initiative (*Centesimus Annus,* #43). So reflection on human rights continues within the tradition of CST and new rights have been asserted since John's 1963 roster. In short, CST offers no fixed and precise list of human rights but has developed a rather comprehensive roster.

In his "address to the 34th General Assembly of the United Nations" (October 2, 1979), John Paul II provided an updated roster of "some of the most important" human rights that the church endorses:

> the right to life, liberty and security of the person; the right to food, clothing, housing, sufficient health care, rest, and leisure; the right to freedom of expression, education and culture; the right to freedom of thought, conscience and religion; the right to manifest one's religion either individually or in community, in public or in private; the right to choose a state of life, to found a family and to enjoy all conditions necessary for family life; the right to property and work, to

adequate working conditions and a just wage; the right of assembly and association; the right to freedom of movement, to internal and external migration; the right to nationality and residence; the right to political participation and the right to participate in the free choice of the political system of the people to which one belongs (#13).

As you can tell, CST embraces a wide array of human rights. It is a list much closer to the U.N. Declaration on Human Rights than those established as constitutional in the United States. While CST maintains that human rights should be recognized by law in all nations, it is aware that, at present, human rights will be moral claims that are only sometimes recognized by civil law. Translating moral rights into legally binding rights is one of the aims of the church's teaching.

27. That's a pretty long list of rights. How does the church decide something is or is not a human right?

That's a tough yet key question to think about. First, there is no simple consensus on what constitutes a human right. CST's list is by no means universally accepted even by members of the church. Second, over the years the church has worked out a structure for rights-language that at least provides a framework for us to discuss, or argue about, human rights.

Traditionally, when Catholicism examines the language of rights it looks to four dimensions of the question. The first is the foundation or basis for a right—what rationale supports the right? For CST the foundation is human dignity. The second dimension is the subject of the right—who has the right? If we are talking about a human right, the subject is each human being. The third is the range of the right—what does it cover or provide? In CST there are both social and economic goods as well as civil and political liberties that are properly understood to be human rights. Finally, there is the duty corresponding to a right. Does the right oblige us to do or refrain from doing something? Who is obliged? An individual? A group? A government agency? All of society?

When making an appeal to human rights each of these four aspects—the foundation, the subject, the range and the duty—must be addressed for a fully satisfactory theory of human rights. Human dignity provides the foundation but does not resolve all the questions about a theory of human rights. We must ask, what does human dignity require in this time and place and what is required of whom?

28. Are you suggesting that as social conditions change a person's human rights change?

The range of human rights supported by the church has developed over the years. This is to be expected as social conditions develop. New threats to human dignity emerge, new means of protecting human dignity become available and new conditions make previously unnecessary goods necessary for dignity. Human rights are not listed in some predetermined manner but by critical reflection on what is required in order to safeguard a person's dignity. If, as CST alleges, human dignity is realized in community, then as the conditions of the community develop so, too, must human rights.

For example, in an earlier age all that could be provided in regard to a right to health care might have been public health measures such as quarantine or basic sanitation. Today, since we can provide more care due to medical advances, we have altered our understanding of what services are included in a right to health care. Or again, in medieval Europe no one would claim that a right to formal education was necessary for personal freedom; in contemporary U.S. society, denial of a basic formal education would seriously undercut a person's ability to participate in communal life and thereby harm his or her dignity.

It is quite understandable that as societies move through preindustrial, industrial and postindustrial stages we will identify new objects of rights and revise what we think ought to be considered as an element of a rights-claim. In one period the threats to human dignity can be primarily political (arbitrary arrest, torture, oppression) while another age may see threats that are more economic in nature (crushing poverty, chronic unemployment, homelessness). Depending on the social conditions, one right may gain cultural acceptance long before another is acknowledged.

29. Why have human rights become so important to CST?

There are at least two ways, strategically and substantively, I can respond. Strategically, John Paul II has pursued an approach that permits him to to proclaim the social message of the gospel to a diverse world. Basically, John Paul II has argued that there is no single pattern of social organization that must be followed. Various nations and cultures can follow different political, economic and social strategies as deemed fitting. But, whatever social order is adapted must be at the service of human rights.

We might see human rights as providing the framework within which societies must operate. This framework does not determine the specifics of social organization and practice but it does set the limits within which a good society functions. In effect, the strategic import of human rights for CST is as the means of articulating a universal message despite the broad array of cultures and social systems found in our world.

The church embraces human rights for the substantive reason that we have come to see the intimate connection between them and human dignity. This is an example of how CST has evolved as a result of its interaction with other political ideas. When nineteenth-century popes heard liberals' cry for personal rights they interpreted this plea, in some cases rightly, as an exaggerated individualism. But as liberalism's understanding of freedom was modified over the course of events the church came to appreciate the centrality of freedom to human dignity. By the time of Vatican II the bishops could state: "Authentic freedom is an exceptional sign of the divine image within the person" (*Gaudium et Spes,* #17).

The church also reflected upon the place of rights-language in explaining the meaning of the common good. In *Pacem in Terris,* John XXIII wrote "in our time the common good is chiefly guaranteed when personal rights and duties are maintained" (#60). Achieving the common good at the expense of the person's rights is a false proposition. Human rights spell out the standards of personal well-being that any conception of the common good must embrace.

D. Common Good

30. Can you explain what is meant by the common good?

This term is often invoked in CST. Perhaps the most commonly cited explanation is John XXIII's succinct description of the common good as "the sum total of conditions of social living, whereby persons are enabled more fully and readily to achieve their own perfection" (*Mater et Magistra,* #65). For CST the common good is not an aggregate term, the totality of individual goods. Rather, there are goods that are only experienced in common, as shared, or they are not experienced at all.

The common good also suggests that the good of each person, the well-being of the human person, is connected to the good of others. That is, human beings only truly flourish in the context of a community. Our well-being is experienced amidst a setting in which other persons also flourish. From this perspective we can say two things: Each of us has an obligation to contribute to the common good so that human life can flourish, and no description of the common good can exclude concern for an individual, writing off some person or group as unworthy of our interest. That is why human rights claims have become an important dimension of the common good in CST; no one should be denied the basic goods needed to join in the life of the community.

The centrality of the common good in CST reflects the communitarian outlook of the tradition, and a commitment to serve the common good is a means whereby the dignity of each person is given its due.

31. When I hear language like "serve the common good" I begin to worry about personal freedom. Some talk about the common good sounds an awful lot like socialism. Isn't the common good a socialist idea?

No, not at all. Of course, a lot depends on how you define your terms but CST draws upon classical sources like Aristotle as well as patristic and medieval sources such as Augustine and Aquinas for the idea of the common good. These far predate the advent of modern socialism. What CST reflects, as I have mentioned previously, is a communitarian outlook which highlights the claims that arise out of social life. It is a way of thinking as old as the prophets when they called upon

Israel to care for the "widow, orphan and alien" or Jesus' parable of the Good Samaritan in which the neighbor is a category broader than most of us would define it.

In the culture of a nation like the United States, where individualism is the ruling presumption, any rival perspective which upholds personal duties and obligations that accrue from the experience of shared life defies the conventional wisdom. As such it can be branded as socialism. Doing so may permit some to dismiss CST as being part of a failed social philosophy like the discredited approaches of twentieth-century communism. That is why it is important to be clear about what we mean.

Extreme renderings of personal freedom or unregulated markets are at odds with appeals to the common good. When properly understood, however, democratic freedoms or market-based economics are not antithetical to the common good. Indeed, the argument of CST is that neglect of the common good leads to the undermining of such political and economic arrangements. Calling attention to the common good is simply a way of pointing out that human beings are not meant for isolation, but are essentially social creatures who achieve their perfection in and through the creation of genuine community where pursuit of the good is a shared endeavor.

32. But who defines what is the common good?

In a nation and world as pluralistic as ours this is a huge issue. Since there is such diversity among people on the matter of what constitutes a good life, how can we avoid using the common good as a rhetorical device that unfairly imposes one vision upon all? Let me make two points by way of response.

It has been said there is unity in misery but diversity in happiness. It is far harder to describe what makes people happy than it is to determine what makes them miserable: the destruction of war; poverty, hunger and disease; injustice and oppression; persecution for dissident beliefs. We might seek consensus on eliminating or at least reducing these evils in any proposal for promoting the common good. From such an approach we may not reach agreement on all the details of a fully developed theory of the common good, but we might be able to articulate a sufficient vision of the good that we can use to guide social policy.

So all talk of the common good does not necessarily lead to imposition of a "one-size-fits-all" definition of the good life that violates respect for the diversity of opinion and belief. And yet, we can find some agreed-upon substantive meaning of the common good.

My second point concerns the means of deliberating about the common good. CST teaches that we can get to some kind of overlapping consensus but the way to it is not through abstract theorizing about human nature. Instead, we employ democratic discussion and debate allowing people to describe and support a particular understanding of the common good.

In another time, one that assumed more paternalistic social organization, we might have presumed that identification and promotion of the common good was the role of the prince or another authority. Some of the earlier writings of CST reflect this assumption but in our present age the church has acknowledged the utility of democratic processes. So CST's answer to the question, "who defines the common good?" is that we do, through active participation in the processes of democratic citizenship.

33. What do you mean by solidarity?

Solidarity is a term that defies neat definition in CST. The *Catechism of the Catholic Church* likens it to "social charity" (#1939). It is a modern term that can make older claims about an organic society and natural sociality understandable to a contemporary audience. Solidarity is more than what is commonly meant by the word interdependence. The fact that we are linked to one another in a variety of ways is interdependence. But individuals may acknowledge this fact while being resentful or indifferent toward it, even as they take advantage of the others with whom they are interconnected. Interdependence does not rule out domination or exploitation.

Solidarity, on the other hand, moves interdependence to another level, beyond acknowledging the fact of interdependence. Solidarity shapes the response we should have to interdependence, evoking within us a desire to build the bonds of common life. As a virtue, solidarity, in the words of John Paul II, is not a feeling of vague compassion but a "firm and persevering determination to commit oneself to the common good" (*Sollicitudo Rei Socialis,* #38). Solidarity shapes the character of a person so that mere recognition of interdependence is transformed into a commitment to the common good. It is solidarity that enables people to devote themselves "to the good of all and of each individual, because we are all really responsible for all" *(Ibid.)*.

Virtues, such as solidarity, shape our character and our actions should flow from our character. Part of what it means to be a person of integrity is that there is a fit between one's personal character and behavior. But we all know that acting on our beliefs can be helped or hindered by the environment in which we find ourselves. For example, it is easier to be cooperative and forgiving when we find ourselves with people who also seek cooperation or are willing to admit their own faults and forgive the errors of others. We can, in short, create social conditions that facilitate solidarity or frustrate it.

34. What is meant by the "preferential option for the poor"?

There are at least three ways in which the expression "preferential option for the poor" can be understood. The first way is as a vision, that is, it has to do with the way we look at and interpret social life.

We know that our perspective on any issue is partial. Things look different if we step outside our usual frame of reference: The experience of cancer is seen differently by the patient, the doctor, a family member of the patient or a medical researcher. So, too, a minimum wage policy will look different to us depending on the perspective from which we view it. The vision suggested by CST encourages us to choose (option) to see first (preferential) how things look to a poor person. This may not be the only way to see things, but it is *a* way of seeing things that CST suggests reveals dimensions of the common good that are often overlooked.

A second way of understanding preferential option for the poor is as a moral concern. It is a reminder that God has always had a special concern for the "widow, orphan and foreigner in the land," that biblical triad which serves as a designation for the weak, vulnerable, poor. When contributing to the common good we ought to attend to the needs of the least advantaged before we turn our attention to the agenda of the better off.

A third way of talking about the preferential option for the poor is as a call to empowerment or liberation. A particular feature of recent CST has been this sensitivity to avoid moral concern being reduced to the "haves" doing for the "have nots." CST maintains that the poor should have a say and an active role in processes that are aimed at improving their situation and building the common good.

In sum, then, the preferential option for the poor entails a way of interpreting social realities, promotes a moral concern and suggests strategies focused on self-determination and empowerment.

E. Justice

35. What does the church mean by justice?

Justice is a word so often used in CST that there should be no surprise it has multiple meanings. Among the most ancient of definitions of justice, and one compatible with usage in CST, is "to render to persons their due." That definition is quite generic; so still to be sorted out is how we are to determine what is due a person. Answering that question introduces us to various theories of justice.

Should we determine what is due someone on the basis of need? Perhaps in some cases such as basic nutrition we would, but in the case of a student needing a passing grade we should be reluctant to see that as a claim of justice. Rather, in the latter case the determination of what is due a person is based on merit. In other situations, such as voting rights, there is a case to be made for strict equality irrespective of merit. We do not give an active citizen more votes than the indifferent, ill-informed citizen.

So there are various ways in which we determine what is due a person. Besides need, merit and equality other commonly employed rationales for assessing what is one's due are those based on effort, social utility, free exchange and strict impartiality (similar cases treated similarly). CST endorses no single approach but develops an understanding of justice that serves human dignity.

In their 1986 pastoral letter on the economy [Economic Justice for All], the bishops of the United States used the term "justice as participation" as a way of articulating the substance of the Catholic tradition. That is, justice requires that a person be able to participate in the community's life, and the various realms of social life should be organized in a manner that fosters active participation by all members of society.

36. Can you say more about "participation" as an approach to justice?

When one reads CST, it is clear that the specifics of policy have changed and attitudes toward a host of ideas such as democracy, human rights, private property and religious liberty have undergone development. But, as I have mentioned (Q. 18) there is a coherence to the tradition if we think in terms of an underlying perspective. That communitarian perspective also gives shape to the theory of justice in CST.

As we have seen, an initial premise of CST is the absolute requirement that the dignity of the human person must be served. But the human person is essentially social so a second premise is that human dignity will be realized in community. And the belief that God's creation is destined for the benefit of all suggests the third premise of a common good that all have a right to share.

These fundamental premises give rise to an approach which maintains that an injustice is done to persons when they are effectively marginalized from community. For instance, if we are speaking of economic community it is easy to see how unemployment or extreme poverty are examples of evils that render it difficult for a person to participate in the economic life of a group. Thus, such evils must be overcome if full economic justice is to exist.

To characterize justice as participation calls our attention to those conditions that must be established if persons are to enter into community and both make their contribution to and draw from the benefits of social existence. For many in the United States, however, justice as participation will sound strange since the connection between the two terms is not immediately evident to the American imagination. The expression does resonate with the biblical tradition on justice that is quite different than the ordinary way justice is viewed in this nation.

37. You said that the biblical meaning of justice is different than the usual way the word is understood by Americans. What do you mean?

One of the great benefits of travel to a foreign country is that we can step outside our usual points of reference and see life in a new way. So often what we take for granted is explained by our cultural location.

If we have grown up and lived only in the United States we have imbibed quite a few assumptions that people of another culture might find odd and certainly not self-evident.

Reading the Bible can be like a visit to a foreign land for it offers a different outlook than the conventional thinking of many of us. Whereas we tend to favor impartiality when determining justice, the Bible provides evidence of God's bias toward the weak and poor. While we often resort to considerations of merit when discussing justice, the God of the Bible looks more at need. There is a strong tradition of property rights in the United States, but the Bible records the ancient ideal of jubilee where land is redistributed. When Americans consider justice it is frequently procedural, that is, we set up fair and impartial rules and whatever emerges as the end result is judged as just. In the scriptures justice is more an end-state; it is the establishment of *shalom,* a community of peace where right relationships are restored.

This is not to argue that the culture of this nation is antibiblical or somehow fundamentally at odds with the Christian vision. I simply wish to point out there is a difference in perspective between how justice is frequently portrayed in the Bible and how many in U.S. society think about justice. The traditions can be mutually enriching for American Catholics. CST, to the extent that it draws upon the biblical tradition, will speak with a voice that challenges what frequently are the conventionally accepted premises of our culture.

38. There seem to be several kinds of justice mentioned in the documents. Can you explain them?

Actually, the history of the theory of justice is quite complicated. CST relies upon a traditional threefold distinction of legal, distributive and commutative justice. Legal justice pertains to the common good and covers those aspects of determining what an individual's responsibility is to the community, be that society or the state. So the obligation to obey laws that serve the common good arises from legal justice. Or the obligation to contribute one's fair share of time, talent and/or money to the common good is due to legal justice. Recently, some have used the expression contributive justice rather than legal justice. The reverse side of legal justice is distributive justice, which addresses the relationship of the community's responsibility to the individual. How are we to apportion the benefits and the burdens that exist in the community? Distributive justice is the aspect of the virtue that rules these decisions. Various approaches to distribution exist but, generally speaking, CST gives prominence to the category of need as the first criterion for assessing fair distribution and one's ability or resources when assessing burdens. So only after the basic needs of all are taken care of should other factors be permitted to influence distribution of goods, and with regard to burdens those who have more are expected to bear more.

Commutative justice is that realm of justice which governs the relationships of individuals to one another. We should remember, however, that a modern corporation is frequently understood as a moral person. Thus, the relationship of an employee to a business may be directed by norms of commutative justice. So fair dealing between employer and employee, between consumer and vendor, between borrower and lender is the sort of relationship that falls under the rubric of commutative justice.

39. You have not mentioned social justice in your comments. Where does the church use the term in its teaching?

The use of this term is an area of debate among scholars who do not agree about its derivation and meaning. Leo XIII did not use the term in *Rerum Novarum.* He employed the traditional categories of distributive and commutative justice when presenting his remedies for the plight of industrial workers. Although the term was given passing reference in some Vatican documents before Pius XI, it was that pope who made it a common term in CST.

Pius first used the term social justice after World War I when he questioned the punitive war reparations imposed by the allied forces upon the axis powers. In the pope's mind such a scheme was shortsighted since the punitive approach strained the economies of the conquered nations. In Pius's opinion the Allied peace demands went further than justice allowed.

Later in *Quadragesimo Anno* and then *Divini Redemptoris* (1937) Pius further developed his understanding of social justice. It became the principle of social governance which guaranteed that each entity within a society would receive the appropriate freedom and resources to perform its task and thereby build up the common good. To violate social justice was to work against the proper ordering and functioning of political, economic and social institutions that make up public life. For Pius XI, it was important to establish that justice governs all social relationships and that the solution to social ills was not to be found simply in charity.

Subsequent popes have frequently appealed to social justice. While exact precision in the way the term is used in CST is not to be found, one theologian has suggested we think of it as a "political virtue," having to do with the "creation of patterns of societal organization and activity" whereby human rights are respected and participation in social life is guaranteed for each person (David Hollenbach, "Modern Catholic Teachings Concerning Justice" in *Justice, Peace, and Human Rights,* pp. 16–33). This corresponds with the revised *Catechism* that sees social justice as governing "the conditions that allow associations or individuals to obtain what is their due" (*Catechism of the Catholic Church,* #1928).

40. Could you say more about social justice and how it relates to the other forms of justice?

Social justice is necessary if we are to have communities where commutative, distributive and legal justice flourish. To assess a topic through the lens of commutative justice requires that we acknowledge also the setting in which the moral actors are situated. For example, the late Monsignor John Cronin, an advisor to the American bishops on economic matters, described a controversy in the late 1950s when he argued that according to commutative justice payment of a living wage was a requirement of all employers. If correct, this argument placed a huge burden on some employers in industries where profit margins were slim or in business sectors that were in recession. Cronin records how he was challenged to rethink his position once he understood that the requirement of a living wage fell under the principle of social justice, not commutative justice. (John Cronin, "Forty Years Later: Reflections and Reminiscences" in a collection of essays on CST edited by C. Curran and R. McCormick, *Readings in Moral Theology: Official Catholic Social Teaching*).

Thus, it was not the individual employer acting in isolation who had to pay a living wage. Rather, it was a duty of society to reorganize economic life so that payment of a living wage was possible by responsible employers, and social assistance would be available to supplement the income of those workers who could not earn such a wage due to inadequate productivity or economic hard times.

Similar sorts of examples about the misreading of obligations could be given about legal justice (requiring an unemployed person to contribute monetarily to the common good) or distributive justice (treating the duty of feeding the hungry as if it fell to an individual acting alone). Without consideration of social justice the burdens placed on individuals or groups to act justly become unwieldy and unrealistic. Social justice is an essential dimension to the moral life since it makes other forms of justice feasible as norms to obey.

41. When I was educated in the Catholic school system I used to hear a lot more about the virtue of charity than justice. What is the relationship of charity to justice?

It is probably true to say that at a popular level most of us heard more about charity than justice. As I noted in response to Q. 2, in many of our schools and parishes the social teaching of the church did not always receive the prominence it deserved although that situation is changing.

Charity is understood in several ways: as a motive for social concern, as a sense of compassion for those less fortunate, as particular acts of kindness such as almsgiving or direct aid to the needy. Various organizations exist that encourage the expression of social charity, for example, the St. Vincent DePaul Society. Many church-affiliated institutions such as hospitals, orphanages, and schools give organized expression to charitable activity.

A common distinction made between charity and justice is to see the former as addressing immediate need through direct aid while the latter looks at longer-term solutions through social analysis and change. Another way of putting it is to see charity as a response to the *effects* of personal and social ills while justice aims at remedying the *causes* of such ills.

Unfortunately, there has been a tendency by some Catholics to denigrate one or the other of these responses to the gospel. There are proponents of justice who dismiss charity as "band-aids" that cover up but do not eradicate the problem. Others who advocate charity see justice activities as political ideology masquerading as religious work or an excuse for not "getting your hands dirty" through direct contact with the poor. These are, of course, foolish and unkind characterizations.

Charity work can bring us into contact with the actual faces of the poor, and it meets the immediate needs of people who suffer. Justice activity provides insight into the way in which personal and social life ought to be structured, thereby lessening the need for charity. Both charity and justice are important responses to the challenge of the gospel, both are praised in CST, and both are needed if we are to build a world where human beings live with dignity.

F. Social Life

42. How is the family envisioned in CST?

In CST the family is the original human society and the foundation of all other social groups. It precedes other social groups including the other great social institution, the state. The family is the fundamental building block of society; it is "the first and essential cell of human society" (*Pacem in Terris,* #16). A person has a fundamental right to choose to marry and to found a family. CST is forceful in its defense of the family that has "at least, equal rights with the State in the choice and pursuit of these things which are needful to its preservation and its just liberty" (*Rerum Novarum,* #10).

People achieve their true growth as persons by entering into the web of relationships. And more than most other forms of social life the family is seen as relating "with greater immediacy to [a person's] innermost nature" (*Gaudium et Spes,* #25). John Paul II has spoken of the family as "the first and fundamental structure" for a wholesome "human ecology" (*Centesimus Annus,* #39).

The family contributes to society in several ways. It is the place where individuals acquire and develop the virtues that inform their lives as citizens, consumers, workers, neighbors. As such the family serves as a "kind of school for deeper humanity" for in it "the various generations come together and help one another to grow wiser and to harmonize personal rights with the other requirements of social life" (*Gaudium et*

Spes, #52). People first learn how to relate to others in public life through their interaction with family members.

Also, as a social unit the family contributes to the betterment of society. Paul VI spoke of the family as "the domestic Church" and meant that "there should be found in every family the various aspects of the entire Church," presumably including its social mission. The family, therefore, is meant to be a community "from which the Gospel radiates" out to the wider society (*Evangelium Nuntiandi,* #71).

43. As someone who works as an economist, it seems to me that part of what explains CST's emphasis on social justice is that the teaching has been formulated in a period when the social sciences have given us new insights into our world. What do you think?

I think you are on to something. As I alluded to in Q. 37, the Bible certainly portrays Yahweh in the Old Testament and the Father of Jesus in the New Testament as a God who is just and who cares deeply about justice in the created order. So the interest of Christians in justice is ancient and firmly rooted in our tradition. That said, it is true that in the nineteenth and twentieth centuries, the period in which the official documents of CST were written, we have seen a vast growth of knowledge in the social sciences. Disciplines like economics, political science, sociology, anthropology and social psychology have made great contributions and also spurred further work in areas such as public administration, business management, leadership training and similar applied skills for understanding and guiding systemic change. This has led to a profound appreciation for the way that human beings are affected by their social environment and how the practices, institutions and structures that make up our social world can be transformed.

The collective impact upon CST of this expansion of our knowledge has been to focus attention not only on individual moral agents but on the social context within which agents make choices and act. And that social context is not a fixed arrangement determined by the fates, natural law or divine command. Rather, the organization of societies is an historically conditioned set of choices by human individuals and groups. As such, these arrangements are open to moral scrutiny and subsequent reform if human beings wish to transform their situations in pursuit of greater justice. Examining the appropriateness of a society's institutional and structural organization becomes a necessary moral responsibility once we are aware that just as we must undergo personal conversion to be disciples so, too, there is a need for social conversion.

44. We need personal conversion because each of us is a sinner. If we need to have social conversion, does that mean society is a sinner?

Contemporary theology would not put it exactly that way but it does talk about social sin or sinful social structures. We know that our social reality is shaped through the interplay of persons and institutions. It is typical of human beings that they produce cultures, but human beings are also shaped by the culture in which they live. We are different kinds of people than would be the case if we lived in another time and place.

Let me offer a common illustration of social sin. People with racial prejudice within their hearts will create cultural institutions and practices that enshrine that interior disposition. Once embodied in a culture, however, racial prejudice is not only enshrined but perpetuated, for people living in the culture now are taught and pass on racial prejudice through the many formal and informal channels that any culture uses to convey its attitudes and values. Racism in the heart will find expression in the laws, advertisements, business practices, housing patterns, public policies and so forth of a society. These cultural elements will reinforce and pass on the racism to new members of the society. To put it another way, what is internal to people will be externalized in their culture and what gets externalized will, in turn, shape the attitudes and values of those living in the culture. There is a constant reciprocal dynamic at work: We change society and are changed by society.

Social sin points out that the evil of sin is not simply remedied by individuals undergoing moral conversion. Human sinfulness lurks in the heart but also in various aspects of the society we create. So if we want to turn away from sin, we must turn away from it in all its dimensions, one of which is the sinful social structures that make up our social world, our culture. Thus, disciples need to work for social transformation or social conversion just as we must strive for personal conversion.

45. I am a little confused. I have heard of original sin and actual sin that is mortal or venial. Where did this social sin idea come from?

My apologies if I confused you. Social sin is a term of fairly recent vintage; it is meant to capture our understanding of one aspect of the mystery of evil. Since you are familiar with the language of original and actual sin let's look at that for a moment.

Original sin presumes no act of the will on our part; we inherit it. But actual sin is different. Remember one of the traditional conditions for mortal sin, a species of actual sin, is that it requires full consent of the will to an evil. So the tradition has used "sin" to name evil that is both voluntary and involuntary. How can we do that? By using modifiers like "original" or "actual" with the word sin to show we are talking about sin in different ways. We are talking about the mystery of evil in both cases but original sin and actual sin are quite different experiences of evil.

What this indicates is that within the Catholic tradition the mystery of evil is understood as so profound that we must use a variety of terms to describe it adequately. So all talk of sin employs analogy. An analogy describes what is similar amidst difference: Love is blind, war is hell, the car is a lemon. These are all examples of analogy.

We use the same word *sin* to describe similar but different realities. Original sin, actual sin, sinful deeds, sinful temptations or attitudes, mortal sin, venial sin, social sin, sinful structures—all these and other expressions are trying to name something similar, the mystery of evil. But the term *sin* alone lacks a certain precision if it can be used to describe all these aspects of evil. So we use the modifier *social* to signify sin in a particular sense, as it is found in the culturally produced practices and institutions of social life.

Four

Political Life

46. Among the key social institutions is the state. What is the role of the state according to CST?

CST has a high view of the state because the state is understood first as an institution that serves the common good. Few things are so clearly expressed in CST as the claim that the state is to protect and promote the common good. Pius XII made the point that "the state, then, has a noble function; that of reviewing, restraining, encouraging all those private initiatives of the citizen which go to make up national life and so directing them to a common end" ("Address to Eighth International Congress of Administrative Sciences," August 5, 1951). John XXIII saw this role as the rationale for the state's very existence: "the whole reason for the existence of civil authorities is the realization of the common good" (*Pacem in Terris,* #54).

Viewing the state this way then leads to a more positive evaluation of its role in social life rather than an outlook that envisions the state as a necessary evil or even an oppressive authority stifling individual freedom. That said, one can still discuss a host of other matters such as the proper role of the state vis-à-vis other social institutions, what form of government is best, what the power of the state is. CST has expressed itself on these matters and has further specified the role of the state. But the key idea is that the state must serve the common good of society.

47. Charging the state with protecting and promoting the common good makes for a pretty expansive description of the state's role in social life, doesn't it?

Yes and no. Remember that the common good is multifaceted in CST, and we ought not assume that any one community can satisfy its achievement. While the goods of political community are essential they are insufficient to encompass all that the common good entails. There remain the goods of family, friendships, religion and other key components of human life.

So while the state is a highly prized and essential form of community it cannot be understood in a totalitarian way. In a society as complex as ours it is apparent that more than the state is needed to realize the common good. It is equally clear in CST, however, that we do need the state. What is being vigorously debated today is what level of state activity and intervention in society is proper. In order to formulate an answer to that question we must assess what forces threaten the basic goods constituting the common good. Surely, CST acknowledges that the state can endanger these goods, but other forces may effectively block participation in communal life and thereby prevent a person from contributing to and enjoying the common good.

It is unwise to rely upon a single ideological premise to settle all cases. Instead, CST proposes several norms that must be held in tension if we are to discern the proper role of the state in society.

48. What are those norms governing the state's role?

Two norms are especially important: subsidiarity and socialization. Regarding subsidiarity, the classic text is from *Quadragesimo Anno*. Pius XI wrote: "It is an injustice and at the same time a grave evil and a disturbance of right order to transfer to the larger and higher collectivity functions which can be performed and provided for by lesser and subordinate bodies" (#79). Put more concretely, the person in need looks to the family for help; if the family is in need one looks to the neighborhood or local community; if it is the town in need one looks to the county; if the county requires assistance one looks to the state; and if the state cannot meet the need one turns to the national government. Thus, recourse for assistance should not automatically be to the national government but there is no opposition to such recourse if circumstances require it.

Subsidiarity reflects CST's opposition to the reduction of human association outside the family to just one form. Subsidiarity prevents any sort of collectivist or totalitarian outlook that permits the state to dominate all other forms of communal life. It is a norm that warns against any state assuming too great a role in public life, but it also warns a state not to fail in fulfilling its duties to promote the common good.

For this latter reason subsidiarity must be balanced by another procedural norm, socialization, described by John XXIII (*Mater et Magistra*,

#59–67) and adopted by Vatican II (*Gaudium et Spes,* #25). Socialization notes that the growing complexity of modern life and the experience of various forms of interdependence result in a tendency to form new organizational structures both public and private. A larger role for the state, then, while not without its dangers, is not wrong in principle. Indeed, it may be necessary to achieve "an appropriate structuring of the human community" (*Mater et Magistra,* #67). The error is to rely upon a single ideological premise to settle all cases (either a simple opposition to government action or the consistent appeal to national government for intervention). Rather, the proper balancing of the two procedural norms of subsidiarity and socialization is to serve solidarity (see Q. 33).

49. Can we summarize subsidiarity to mean that "smaller is better" or "the less government the better"?

Not exactly, although some have tried to use it that way, as an argument against government. That would, of course, contradict what has just been said about the state being a highly prized social institution in CST. The Latin root of the word is the noun *subsidium* which means help, aid or support. In other words, the principle of subsidiarity has to do with the degree of aid or assistance needed in order to accomplish a task or meet an obligation.

In CST the idea is that one should seek assistance at the closest level to the agent or agency in need. When a smaller social unit is either unable or unwilling to meet the obligation it becomes necessary to turn to the larger social unit. Some agents are simply overwhelmed by a need or a problem and require the resources of a larger social entity. For example, it is doubtful that even extended families can address social problems such as street crime or drug trafficking. Larger social institutions must be utilized.

At other times, an agent is able but simply refuses to satisfy reasonable expectations and a larger social agency must intervene. This is precisely what happened in the U.S. civil rights struggle when some southern states refused to enforce desegregation policies. In response the federal government stepped in to correct unjust practices.

Instead of "the less government the better" the principle might be better summarized as "no bigger than necessary, no smaller than appropriate."

50. I understand what you have been saying, but the impression I have is that church teaching endorses a large role for the state in economic affairs. Is that not so?

In his time Leo XIII was much troubled by the failure of European governments to act responsibly in the face of threats to the common good. Leo makes the case in *Rerum Novarum* that the state must be willing to regulate and intervene in market exchanges that threaten the common good. This right to intervene is not an ad hoc invention by Leo but something that flows from the inner logic of CST on the nature and role of the state. The state must serve the common good and economic prosperity is an integral part of the common good.

The papacy operates, therefore, with a clear premise that the state has the right to intervene in the economic order. No subsequent pope has disagreed with the position adopted by Leo, but what has happened is that there has been ongoing reflection on the extent of the state's right to intervene. Remember, Leo was writing at a time of vocal resistance to an activist state so he wished to make clear the right of the state. Later popes wrote in different settings and so perceived different concerns. By the time Pius XI and Pius XII wrote, the papacy was aware of a new threat to the common good, an omnicompetent state with totalitarian ambitions, and they wished to point out the limits of state action.

So we can see subsidiarity as a way of nuancing the argument espoused by Leo that the state had not only the right but the duty to intervene in economic matters. It is a duty and right but these are not to be understood as absolute. Rather, state intervention must be bounded by the obligation to respect other legitimate public associations that are not only familial and educational but also economic and cultural. The role of the state is determined by its nature: to serve the common good.

In a society as complex as ours it is apparent that more than the state is necessary for realizing the common good; it is equally clear, however, that we do need the state to act in the economic order for the sake of the common good.

51. What, then, does the church say about big government programs such as food stamps or public housing?

Given what we have said about human rights (Q. 26–29) the first thing to say is that the basic needs of people for things such as food or housing must be addressed. But should it be the federal government's role? Throughout the tradition there is a consistent acknowledgment that the nation-state can effectively lessen the impact of economic inequality and social power through regulation and social programs, and this may be necessary.

Balancing this insight is the statement of John Paul II that even in its well-intentioned activity the state may undercut the role of other communities such as family, neighborhood and other voluntary associations. He sees a risk that "the social assistance state leads to a loss of human energies and an inordinate increase of public agencies which are dominated more by bureaucratic ways of thinking than by concern for serving their clients." The pope goes on to say: "It would appear that needs are best understood and satisfied by people who are closest to them and who act as neighbors to those in need." His conclusion is that many people in need "can be helped effectively only by those who offer them genuine fraternal support, in addition to the necessary care" (*Centesimus Annus,* #48).

The communitarian outlook of the pope leads him to question if the size and structure of the welfare state make it the best way to provide social aid in each case. We need not presume the opposite, however, that nonfederal government structures are always to be preferred. Nor should we confuse the delivery of social services with the funding of them. National government may be appropriate as the funding mechanism even when it does not directly provide the services that it funds.

52. What do you mean that the pope's communitarianism influences his view of the welfare state?

When John Paul II writes of the social assistance state he has in mind what many in our culture call the welfare state. Evident throughout his contemporary assessment of that form of government is the persistence of the communitarian outlook. First, there is the charge that large bureaucratic structures are alienating and that governmental bureaucracy is no more humane than the bureaucracies of other large social institutions. Desired is an approach to social action planned on a more human scale.

A second communitarian theme is the value of locally based service agencies. It is likely that institutions which are closer to the grass roots than large governmental offices are better able to deliver services that address the concerns of people.

The third communitarian theme in recent teaching is that more than material needs must be addressed. People in any society do not live by bread alone even if bread is essential. The values humans cherish include those that are found in the experience of being in relationship with others. Here the essential nature of human life as social and society as an organic community of communities determines the appropriate response.

Participation in a wide array of communities allows a person to experience social life through "interrelationships on many levels" and it is "intermediate communities" that give human scale to mass society, offering an alternative to the person who is "often suffocated between two poles represented by the state and the marketplace" (*Centesimus Annus,* #49). So John Paul II believes that an unregulated market can lead to injustice that oppresses, but an unchecked state can also stifle the human spirit. The antidote is the creation of genuine human communities in which every person can find appropriate avenues for mutuality and development. We can see in the pope's words the idea that subsidiarity does not require an antistate stance; what it does require is a strategy to maximize participation. It is hoped that from such opportunities for participation the reality of interdependence will be elevated to the experience of solidarity.

53. With all this talk about participation, I conclude that CST is a strong defender of political democracy as the best form of government. Am I correct?

There is a history concerning the relationship of the Catholic Church to democracy that is quite complicated and filled with left turns, right turns and a few U-turns! And the actual practice of the church has not always been the same as its formal teaching. For our purposes a few points should be made.

The state derives necessarily from the social nature of human beings. Given that our nature is not accidental but reflective of God's plan, one can say by extension that there is a certain divine sanction to the state. But, not the state in any specific concrete manifestation; in the particulars of history the state is a creation of human beings. Society requires authority but the precise institutional expression of such authority is not divinely dictated. Within CST there has been an evolution in grasping what historical forms of the state satisfy the normative idea of a good state. Monarchy, aristocracy, democracy have all been suggested as acceptable and at different times one or the other has been deemed preferable. A certain uneasiness with democracy was due to the fear that it really meant a "mob-ocracy," a tyranny of the majority. As decades passed the papal stance softened, and by the end of the pontificate of Pius XII there was clear support for democracy as the most apt form of government.

Pius was influenced in his view by the threats posed to human dignity in fascism and communism and the alternative offered by western democracies. Subsequent popes have continued and strengthened the preference for democracy. The claim is not that democracy is always and everywhere the ideal form of government but simply that it is most suitable given modernity's emphasis on self-determination, freedom and equality.

A major contention of CST is the insistence that all authority rests originally and finally on God and not on the citizenry. This claim is aimed at avoiding the kind of mob rule where majorities would override moral rights and duties. Thus, constitutionally limited democracies that protect minorities and restrict the powers of the majority are judged to be in accord with CST.

FIVE

ECONOMIC LIFE

54. What occasioned Leo XIII's writing on the economic situation?

It was clear to Leo at the time he wrote *Rerum Novarum* that the laboring class was in a position of grave suffering and extreme threat. That is why at the end of his letter he wrote: "At this moment the condition of the working population is the question of the hour" (#44).

The Latin words *rerum novarum* mean *of new things*. In the opening paragraph Leo described what he saw as "a spirit of revolutionary change" that had passed beyond politics into economic life (#1). Basically, what Leo described were the radically altered circumstances of life as much of Europe moved from a rural agrarian lifestyle to an urban industrial one. The dramatically transformed situation was marked by great social dislocation and suffering during the era of transition. Leo was aware of "new things" and his reading of the situation was that one particular group, and a large one, bore the heaviest burden of the change: industrial workers and the urban unemployed.

For Leo, the social question was not merely economic but also moral and religious. If the economic situation improved and workers lost sight of God and proper ethical standards then nothing would be gained (*Graves de Communi,* #11). There was an evangelical concern in the pope's reading of the situation. Many of the new industrial workers had become alienated from the church once they had left behind the familiar setting of small villages and towns with a local parish. In the teeming cities of the nineteenth century, the church was not as visibly present nor as in touch with the rhythms of everyday life. As a result Catholicism appeared to be irrelevant to the concerns of the burgeoning class of workers. Leo wanted to right that situation by placing the church on the side of those voicing concern for workers thereby making the church attractive to the many who had lost touch with their faith.

55. If it is the plight of workers that CST first addressed, how does the tradition understand the experience of work?

Over the centuries work has been seen in a variety of ways by the Christian community. CST has generally tried to respect the complexity of the phenomenon even as it brings some themes to the foreground.

Despite varying emphases, there are certain themes that can and should be noted in an adequate theology of work. There is the penitential theme of work; often we are exhausted, bored, pained by our labor. One need not take the ancient view that work is a result of the Fall—a punishment imposed upon Adam and Eve and their descendants—to acknowledge that there are harsh and difficult elements to the phenomenon of work. In terms of spirituality, thinking along these lines encourages attention to work as self-discipline, as a means of chastising our bodies and spirits, and as a way of overcoming temptations to idleness and pride.

Another line of thinking within the tradition can view work as a means of preparation, making the world ready for the coming of Christ. Theologically, we might call this an eschatological (pertaining to the "last things") viewpoint. Our work has a thrust toward the future; we are engaged in activity in the hope of at least setting the stage for, if not hastening, the triumphant return of Christ. Human action and God's reign are in sync; there is a continuity between the kingdom of God and the honest labor of people to improve the world.

Spiritually, this outlook can promote a special concern for work as an energetic effort to serve the church and society. Sometimes the thrust may be to do work that explicitly spreads the gospel message or expands the church's presence. At other times the focal point might be to build a more just society, to overcome divisions and war, to heal relationships. But in either case the human effort is viewed from the perspective of the hoped-for final reign of Christ over all creation.

56. I have read that John Paul II did manual labor before he became a priest. Does he have any particular views on human work?

Without doubt the most developed reflection in CST on work's meaning is to be found in John Paul's *Laborem Exercens*. This letter written for the ninetieth anniversary of *Rerum Novarum* is an extended philosophical and theological meditation on human labor that the pope calls "the essential key to the whole social question" (*Laborem Exercens,* #3).

Work can be understood in two ways; it is the means whereby human beings create their social world (the objective sense) and achieve their self-development (the subjective sense) (#5 & 6). Without denying the importance of the objective sense of work, as the way we humanize the world, it is the subjective sense that gives work its real dignity. The way to determine "the value of human work is not primarily the kind of work being done, but the fact that the one who is doing it is a person." Work is for the person, not the person for work. Thus, asserts John Paul, there is a "preeminence of the subjective meaning of work over the objective one" (#6).

The modern error regarding work is see labor as a sort of merchandise that the laborer sells to the employer. This is to invert the proper order of valuation for it gives too much of a role to the objective dimension over the subjective (#7). Historically, John Paul believes the era of industrial capitalism was particularly tempted to distort the right order of valuing work. It is a fundamental error of what John Paul calls "economism" to see labor "solely according to its economic purpose" for this means the humanistic dimension of labor is overlooked: Work is for the development of the human subject (#13 & 15).

Another perspective on work developed by John Paul II is its spirituality, where the human laborer is understood to be continuing the work of God by shaping and transforming the world. Work is a participation in the creative activity of God and human beings can be viewed as co-creators through their ongoing labor (#25).

57. I'm not sure I understand this idea of "co-creation." Can you say a little more about it?

In the twentieth century, a line of reasoning that might be called creational has emphasized work as co-creation, that is, it is through work that human beings both shape and build the world. In doing so they fulfill the mandate of Genesis where Yahweh calls humankind to serve as a faithful steward of God's creation. At another level work is also the means whereby persons develop themselves. So also in this way men and women participate in God's ongoing creative activity fashioning both the world about them and themselves. It is in this way that we can speak of ourselves as co-creators; acting in concert with God's grace, humanity exercises a creative role in the historical development of ourselves, our society, our world.

The spirituality of co-creation should not ignore the penitential and eschatological aspects but it highlights two other dimensions of a Christian understanding of work. Through our freedom and self-awareness, God has invited us into a unique relationship that allows us to see our work as more than just meeting our own needs. Humanity's role in the plan of creation is to cooperate with the Creator in fashioning a created order that reflects the grandeur and purpose of God.

Second, our work, whatever it is, has the element of a personal calling, a vocation. We ought to discern, develop and direct our personal talents and gifts so that the work we do becomes both a response to God's call and a means of following Christ. For men and women to be good workers is as much a way of discipleship as being a good spouse, parent or friend.

58. How does the church view labor unions?

The quick answer to your question is "favorably," an answer that does not do complete justice to the long history of the church and the labor movement. There have been criticisms of specific unions, of certain tactics and practices of unions, and of the social dangers when unions foster class division and conflict. But, even with that said, it is clear that the idea of workers uniting in solidarity to protect their rights and pursue worthy social goods is defended as a basic right in CST.

Leo XIII approved of labor associations in *Rerum Novarum* (#36–38), defending them as being both necessary and highly advantageous. Subsequent popes have endorsed this claim. The idea of labor unions finds support both in the Catholic affirmation of the social nature of the person and in the political theory of CST that defends subsidiarity and the significant place to be given to voluntary associations in the attainment of the common good. Human beings ought to join together to realize mutually beneficial goals and this holds true for the particular class of humans we call workers. And society as a whole benefits when a variety of human organizations flourish between the realms of the private individual and of the state.

59. You mentioned there have been criticisms of labor unions in CST. What are they?

CST does contain some reservations or criticisms of the labor movement, or better put, of a distorted version of a labor movement. These can be summarized under four broad headings and the concerns are often more relevant to one time period or one geographic region than another. First is the risk of a truly polarized society in which feelings of enmity are encouraged by divisive forces and where means as extreme as violence are employed in the contest for power. Second is the danger that Catholic workers will lose a sense of their religious identity or even the virtue of faith due to alliances and allegiances within a secular organization. A third problem in the mind of some authors within CST is that a labor movement may become a political party that seeks to advance the interests of one class against others, and which narrowly defines the purposes of politics to interest-group activity instead of the common good. Finally, a fourth misunderstanding of labor unions is to use the power of organized labor to dominate all other economic factors. Making wage or other demands that neglect the legitimate concerns and needs of employers, managers, consumers and so forth is an abuse.

These reservations, which can be found in one or another statement of CST, do not lead to opposition toward organized labor. If anything, these concerns have led the church to encourage active engagement in the labor movement by Catholics so as to avoid the errors just enumerated. But it is not just avoidance of errors that should motivate Catholics to join the labor movement. Both in theory and in practice, CST has seen the organized labor movement as a positive force for social change, for protection of basic rights and the common good.

60. Among the basic rights of labor which CST has proposed is that of a just wage. What is meant by a just wage?

This expression, a just wage, is also termed within the tradition a living wage, a family wage or just compensation. It is a fundamental teaching of CST for it is closely linked to human dignity. People have a legitimate claim based on their dignity to those essential material goods that meet basic needs for food, clothing, shelter, health, education, security and rest—this is the minimum condition of wage-justice. Ordinarily, it is to be expected that an able-bodied person will obtain the basic goods through labor, either as the fruit of one's work or in exchange for it. This is a long-standing presumption within the tradition.

By the time of Leo XIII, however, this presumption had been undercut due to the working of the labor market in the emergent industrial order. Classical liberalism's defense of free markets included the principle of free contract, that is, a just contract was one that the signees entered into freely. In practice, this meant many workers desperate for a position took jobs for paltry wages that were inadequate for meeting basic needs for themselves and their dependents. Leo forthrightly criticized such an approach and challenged the doctrine of free contract by asserting that justice, not freedom, is the governing norm of contracts. And justice, rooted in human dignity, meant that a just wage is one which allows a worker and family to live in "reasonable and frugal comfort" (*Rerum Novarum*, #34).

Later popes such as Pius XI and John XXIII have acknowledged that determination of a just wage entails assessment of specific and concrete social conditions: the fiscal health of the business, the cost of living, market forces, the role of other actors—local, national and international. There is no fixed, one size-fits-all approach to defining a just wage. But the conviction is that wages must be determined by more than free consent of the contractual parties. As such, concern for justice and rights must be factored into determination of what constitutes a just wage.

61. What exactly is the view of the church regarding poverty?

The first thing to be said about poverty is that "in God's sight poverty is no disgrace" for "the true dignity and excellence of the person lies in moral qualities, that is, in virtue" and the poor no less than others are capable of virtue (*Rerum Novarum,* #20).

Certain quarters within American life have promoted a "gospel of wealth" in which it is believed God abundantly blesses the labors of the good. The logic of this claim is then reversed in some instances to mean that if one had material abundance one was good. From here it is a small step to consider those without wealth to be morally lacking. But CST will have none of that.

On the matter of poverty we must distinguish between what is voluntary and involuntary. When poverty is voluntarily assumed, such as a member of a religious community taking a vow of poverty, the church sees it as good. Involuntary poverty, however, is not a blessing but something to be overcome.

From the New Testament portrayal of the early church to the witness of medieval monastic and mendicant communities to the social works provided by organizations such as the Vincent DePaul Society—history is replete with examples of believers offering assistance to those in poverty. The vast array of social services that the church sponsors bears testimony to Leo XIII's claim: "its [the Church's] desire is that the poor...should rise above poverty and wretchedness, and should better their condition in life; and for this it strives" (*Rerum Novarum,* #23).

It is rare, though not unheard of, for the church to encounter criticism for its direct services on behalf of the poor. But attacking the causes of poverty invites more criticism because people disagree about the nature of the causes as well as the most appropriate remedies. Such debates can be welcome if they lead to greater insight. What should not be debated is the obligation the Christian community has to care for the poor and the importance of the church's social action in opposing poverty so that the basic material needs of people are satisfied.

62. A lot of attention with talk of a just wage and the care of the poor seems to be about a floor below which people should not fall, but does CST talk about a ceiling above which people should not rise?

Not in so many words, but there are clear indications that CST operates with the assumption that people can have more than is good for themselves, others and the world. This can be seen in comments in the documents about true and false development, about the duty of charity and, more recently, about threats to the environment.

CST is critical of consumerism. In *Centesimus Annus* one finds John Paul II stating: "It is not wrong to want to live better; what is wrong is a style of life which is presumed to be better when it is directed toward 'having' rather than 'being'" (#36). Another way of stating this problem is found in John Paul's criticism of "superdevelopment," which is "an excessive availability of every kind of material goods" that "easily makes people slaves of 'possession' and of immediate gratification" (*Sollicitudo Rei Socialis,* #28).

When we consider the duty of charity, CST distinguishes between categories of material well-being, for example basic versus luxury goods. At Vatican II when the bishops retrieved the patristic ideal of giving out of one's substance and not just from what is superfluous, they were appealing to the faithful to donate a portion of those goods that go beyond merely luxury items when confronted by the dire poverty of those without even basic goods (*Gaudium et Spes,* #69).

Recent comments on the state of the environment show John Paul II to be worried that our earth cannot continue to endure a lifestyle in which humanity "consumes the resources of the earth…in an excessive and disordered way" (*Centesimus Annus,* #37). Earlier, in his 1990 World Day of Peace Statement, the pope made the point directly: "Modern society will find no solution to the ecological problem unless it *takes a serious look at its lifestyle"*(*The Ecological Crisis: A Common Responsibility,* #13, emphasis in original).

When one reflects on such statements, it seems fair to say that while there is no specific limit on material possessions we certainly find in CST concern that we can have too much.

63. I'd like to get a bit more specific. How much of one's goods ought to be donated in charity?

CST does not propose norms that specify an exact amount. Norms are cited to make clear that an obligation exists to give out of one's excess regularly, and in cases of extreme need to be prepared to give all of one's excess and even to forego a measure of the ordinary and modest comfort to which one has become accustomed.

In our situation, discernment of the proper proportion of a person's wealth to be given away is not easily generalized. No one personal or family situation will be identical to another and financial decisions are affected by both personal and social contexts. Saving money in order to provide for a family means one thing if an only child wishes to pursue a manual trade and quite another if several children all wish to enter college. No fixed formula for determination of how much to give will be sensitive to the differences among people.

The tradition offers the negative warning of idolatry and the positive ideal of solidarity. Negatively, we ought not permit our attachment to wealth and possessions to stand in the way of our relationship with the God who loves the poor. Positively, we must remember the words of John XXIII quoted at Vatican II: "The obligation of every person, the urgent obligation of the Christian, is to reckon what is superfluous by the measure of the needs of others" (*Gaudium et Spes,* fn. 147).

Whatever choices are to be made, CST is clear that discipleship is intimately linked to charity. If disciples regularly develop budgets and lifestyles where no surplus is identified, then self-examination is needed. Recall that even the poor are expected to share what little they have as the gospel story of the widow's mite illustrates. To expend all, or almost all, our resources on ourselves is to ignore the fact of poverty for it effectively means that we will live as if the poor make no claim upon us. Such an operational standard clearly violates a fundamental element of Christian discipleship that is valid for any age.

64. Is the church's teaching on capitalism one of approval or disapproval?

This is one of those questions where the answer can only be given once it is clear what is meant by capitalism. John Paul II put the question to himself about whether capitalism is a model to be followed. He answered: "If by capitalism is meant an economic system which recognizes the fundamental and positive role of business, the market, private property and the resulting responsibility for the means of production, as well as free human creativity in the economic sector, then the answer is certainly in the affirmative..." (*Centesimus Annus,* #42). So clearly there is an understanding of capitalism that the church approves.

On the other hand, John Paul also stated: "But if by capitalism is meant a system in which freedom in the economic sector is not circumscribed within a strong juridical framework which places it at the service of human freedom in its totality, and which sees it as a particular aspect of that freedom, the core of which is ethical and religious, then the reply is certainly negative" (*Ibid.*). Very much in keeping with the legacy of CST, John Paul is wary of a capitalism which exalts freedom to the extent that justice, rights, the common good and human dignity are sacrificed. This is why he stipulates that economic freedom be understood in the context of a "strong juridical framework." A false capitalism takes one part of human freedom, economic liberty, and makes of it the whole story.

Within CST there is an appreciation for the utility and virtues of a market economy. But this fundamental acceptance of a free market economic model is always tempered by concerns that self-interest not override the common good, that unregulated freedom not lead to exploitation of others or of creation, that appreciation for material prosperity not create false understandings of human development and well-being.

Perhaps a fair summary of the position of CST on capitalism is that it gets a conditional approval; it is not inherently wrong but false renderings of capitalist economics, which have existed in the past and continue in the present, must be opposed.

65. If capitalism gets a conditional approval, what are the conditions?

One can comb through the documents of CST and find a list of ills in capitalism to be remedied. It is possible to arrange the list of papal concerns under four headings: (a) establishment by the state of a juridical framework to regulate market operations, (b) communal provision of basic goods/services for all, (c) promotion of personal and group morality, and, finally, (d) protection of voluntary associations and other elements of civil society (Daniel Finn, "John Paul II and the Moral Ecology of Markets" in *Theological Studies,* vol. 59 [1998] pp. 662–79).

Juridical framework means that government must establish fair and wise regulations that permit markets to function optimally for human well-being while still respecting individual freedom. Second, any economy must see to it that no one is deprived of essential goods or services because of not having sufficient capital. However the economy operates, it must have in place a means whereby the community can guarantee that a person's basic material needs are satisfied.

Despite good laws and structures there remains a large role to be played by morally virtuous people. Honesty, diligent work, compassion, generosity, creativity, thoughtfulness, friendship—these and many other virtues are not things that can be legislated but without them neither market economies nor human societies are sustainable. A sound economic system will not undercut the very qualities of character in persons and groups that make social life possible.

One of the dangers in modern times is that market forces are being extended into areas of life where they do not belong. Just as the extension of government into all realms of social existence violates the principle of subsidiarity so, too, something similar can be said about economic markets. It is important that social groupings of family, church, neighborhood, fraternal and sororal clubs, recreational and educational organizations and the like should function by their own logic and ethos, not that of the market.

Without suggesting a detailed blueprint for building a just economy, these four categories of John Paul's offer an analytic framework for naming CST's conditions for approval of a capitalist economy.

66. What about the papal view of private property? Is it critical or approving?

Throughout CST there is strong support for the institution of private property. One finds in Leo XIII's *Rerum Novarum* perhaps the strongest affirmation of private property "as being in conformity with human nature" (#8). This is due in part to the pope's criticism of socialism and his interest in distinguishing CST's criticism of capitalist abuses in the nineteenth century from Marxist or socialist criticisms.

Private property serves several worthwhile ends according to CST. It permits workers to meet their basic temporal needs; it also allows workers to gain some financial stability for their families; it offers security for the future, especially in old age; it rewards hard work and frugality; it serves as a means of protecting personal liberty; it permits workers to be creative and to exercise self-determination. In addition, the social institution of private property is a useful way to see to it that people will assume responsibility for the proper care of God's creation (#5–7).

A right of possession of property, however, ought not be equated with right of use. People may abuse their possessions and use them improperly. Such abuse should be challenged and may even be restrained for the common good: "Public authority, in view of the common good, may specify more accurately what is licit and what is illicit for property owners in the use of their possessions" (#49). Abuse does not cancel the right of private property ownership. The corollary of this is also true; regulation of use does not violate the right of ownership of private property *(Ibid.)*.

The popes were aware that the existing laws and customs regarding ownership of private property were hardly ideal. Their approach was to temper the abuses without seeking abolition of the principle of private ownership. In their view this was the extreme remedy that the socialists wrongly pursued.

67. Has the teaching on private property evolved over the years?

Yes, basically the development has been in the direction of underscoring the social dimension of private property. Pius XI affirmed the "twofold aspect of ownership, which is individual or social accordingly as it regards individuals or concerns of the common good" (*Quadragesimo Anno*, #45). Pius XII retrieved the patristic theme of the universal destiny of all goods as the context for thinking about private property *(June 1, 1941 Pentecost Address)*. There can be a diversity of ownership schemes that should be left to particular customs and statutes of a society. Any such scheme "remains subordinated to the natural scope of material goods and cannot emancipate itself from the first and fundamental right which concedes their use to all" *(Ibid.)*.

In effect, the raising up of the social dimensions of ownership has led CST to insist not only on the individual right of private property but the "social duty essentially inherent in the right" (*Pacem in Terris*, #22).

Paul VI explicitly denied that the right to private property can be considered "an absolute and unconditioned right" for "the right to private property must never be exercised to the detriment of the common good" (*Populorum Progressio*, #23). This principle extends to the case that "the common good sometimes demands expropriation" (#24).

According to John Paul II all property has a "'social mortgage,' meaning it has an intrinsically social function based upon and justified precisely by the principle of the universal destination of goods" (*Sollicitudo Rei Socialis*, #42). While it remains true private property is a right that is *"valid and necessary"* it is important in the face of widespread poverty to affirm "the characteristic principle of Christian social doctrine: the goods of this world are *originally meant for all"* (*Ibid.*, italics in original).

68. Considering Leo's opposition to socialism, does the church distinguish between socialism and communism?

In Leo's writing the word socialism covered a multitude of bad ideas and social movements. What gets lumped together under the name of socialism are all those who argue against private property, advocate class conflict, support a collectivist state and are antireligious.

Pius XI distinguished between two types of socialism (*Quadragesimo Anno,* #112–20). One type "has degenerated into 'communism'" that "shows itself cruel and inhuman in a manner unbelievable and monstrous" (#112). The other type, "which has retained the name of 'socialism,'" is much less radical in its views. By the time Pius XI was writing, he had witnessed Lenin and the 1917 revolution as well as the rise of Stalinism; Pius saw the evils of an actual communist state. His criticism was both clear and uncompromising in the encyclical *Divini Redemptoris,* promulgated in 1937.

Yet Pius saw another development on the left besides the totalitarianism of communism. This moderate school eventually emerged as the democratic socialist parties in countries such as Germany and France. But the evolution was incomplete and in the end the papal judgment of even moderate socialism was that "no one can be at the same time a sincere Catholic and a true socialist" (*Quadragesimo Anno,* #120).

Later popes continued to refine and nuance the judgment of socialism in CST. John XXIII in 1963 wrote that it was important "to make a clear distinction between false philosophical teachings regarding the nature, origin, and destiny of the universe and of the human, and movements which have a direct bearing either on economic and social questions, or cultural matters or on the organization of the state, even if these movements owe their origin and inspiration to these false tenets" (*Pacem in Terris,* #159).

During the pontificates of Paul VI and John Paul II, some socialist criticisms of capitalist economics have been integrated into CST although there remains a concern that the social analysis is not easily separated from an underlying philosophical world view inimical to faith and religion.

69. One of the most important institutions in modern capitalism is the corporation. What do we find about corporations in CST?

There is no fundamental opposition to the idea of the corporation in CST but there are concerns. Due to the size and impersonality of corporations personal responsibility and accountability may become obscure. Ownership of private property carries with it social duties. Frequently, the owners of corporations are stockholders who have little direct role in the practices of the corporation. Real decision-making occurs at the levels of the board of directors and the professional managers they hire. In a structure of committees and task forces, it is not always clear even to participants just whose voice or vote was crucial in determining a course of action. Pius XI attacked the manner in which corporations, "with their divided responsibility and limited liability, have given occasion to abominable abuses....The worst injustice and frauds take place beneath the obscurity of the common name of a corporate firm" (*Quadragesimo Anno,* #132).

Pius XII was the pope most prone to look skeptically at the growth in size of modern institutions. While Pius saw danger in the expansion of government activity in people's lives, he also frowned upon the power and cultural impact of the large corporation. "It is right for the world to admire enterprises which in the area of production and management succeed in coordinating and mobilizing the physical forces of men and matter....But what must be denied is that modern social life should be regulated by them or made to conform to them" *(1952 Christmas Address).*

Despite these warnings, CST approaches the modern business corporation with an attitude that the power, productivity and influence of corporations can be used to bring about much good both for those within and outside the corporation. The concerns voiced should not be interpreted as antibusiness. But the documents of CST do demonstrate a consistent interest that some sort of framework be established which provides for a structure of accountability to examine the decisions and activities of stockholders, directors and managers within the complex institution of the modern corporation.

70. Is there anything in CST on the phenomenon of multinational or transnational corporations?

It is precisely the issues of power and lack of accountability that concerned Paul VI who wondered by what rules large transnational corporations are governed. "Under the driving force of new systems of production, national frontiers are breaking down, and we can see new economic powers emerging, the multinational enterprises, which by the concentration and flexibility of their means can conduct autonomous strategies which are largely independent of the national political powers and therefore not subject to control from the point of view of the common good" (*Octogesima Adveniens,* #44).

Recall the important role CST gives to the state for promotion and protection of the common good. Once corporations have become transnational, the obvious question arises about who can enforce appropriate regulation that would ensure attention is given to the common good. This is particularly worrisome when the majority of stockholders, directors and managers of a corporation are not residents of the nation where the corporation is located. And it is, of course, many of the poorer nations where this situation pertains. That is why John Paul II warned that while economic interdependence is "in itself normal" it yet may "become an occasion for various forms of exploitation or injustice" (*Laborem Exercens,* #17). He went on to cite transnational companies specifically as one of the causes for the ever-widening gap between rich and poor in the world.

It is also true that transnational corporations can bring capital investment, useful technology, stable wages, new products and knowledge to poor nations and regions. CST does not teach that transnational corporations are inherently bad, only that the emergence of these economic institutions calls for the creation of new styles of cooperation between governments and private economic participants.

As a consequence, CST calls for "codes of conduct" whereby some measure of regulation is available, standards of behavior are established and the larger social responsibility of the corporation is acknowledged. Without such codes the power of transnational corporations will not bring good things to host countries but participate in a new kind of economic colonialism (*Populorum Progressio,* #52).

71. I'm a "white-collar" worker who doesn't own the company where I am employed. Does the church have anything to say directly to individuals who work in corporations as managers?

To my mind, the document that has best addressed the managerial role is the 1986 pastoral letter of the American bishops, *Economic Justice for All.*

First, the bishops affirm that the labor of corporate "white-collar" workers, like all work, has a "threefold moral significance." It is a chief way in which "people exercise the distinctive human capacity for self-expression and self-realization." Work is also the "ordinary way for human beings to fulfill their material needs." And, importantly, "work enables people to contribute to the well-being of the larger community" (#97).

Quoting from a speech of John Paul II, the bishops write that social well-being would be "unthinkable without the dynamic figure of the business person, whose function consists of organizing human labor and the means of production" so as to build prosperity and advance progress (#108). Managerial workers have duties to the corporation and its stockholders but this does not exhaust their responsibilities. "Commitment to the public good and not simply the private good of their firms is at the heart of what it means to call their work a vocation and not simply a career or a job" (#109).

People charged with leadership and management of modern corporations fulfill a stewardship role and must demonstrate prudent judgment in the use of human resources as well as material goods such as financial capital, natural resources and the physical environment. Short-term profit-taking at the expense of these goods can be morally shortsighted (#110). In many cases, retired workers, local communities and business partners have aided in the success of a corporation. Managers must have a broad vision of their responsibility and the audience to whom they are accountable (#111). In particular, CST envisions a cooperative relation between workers and management.

Using the tools and skills at their command, managers serve a valuable role in the modern economy and when done with a commitment to serve the common good managers transform their jobs into vocations.

72. I think it is fair to say that CST was formulated in an age of industrial labor and agricultural work. What can CST say to people employed in a postindustrial economy, whether we call it an "information society" or a "service economy"?

In his reflection on human work John Paul II wrote, "Both the original industrialization that gave rise to what is called the worker question and the subsequent industrial and post-industrial changes show in an eloquent manner that, even in the age of ever more mechanized 'work,' the proper subject of work continues to be the human person" (*Laborem Exercens,* #5). Thus, in CST the focus remains on the human experience of work even as the kind and manner of work change. This permits the tradition to use human dignity as the baseline for examining the world of work even as that world undergoes many developments.

Technology is described as "undoubtedly humankind's ally" that "perfects, accelerates and augments" human labor *(Ibid.).* It is viewed as a means of improving both the quantity and quality of human production. But "in some instances technology can cease to be the person's ally and become almost an enemy" by "taking away personal satisfaction and the incentive to creativity and responsibility"....In the transition to new forms of technology jobs can be lost and machines can be prized above people *(Ibid.).*

While the nature of the economy in nations like the United States is undergoing dramatic alteration, these changes are seen in CST as neither cause for despair nor uncritical optimism. Human dignity, human rights, the common good—these remain touchstones for CST to scrutinize the emerging economies of the postindustrial societies.

73. Not everyone works at computer stations or in marketing, sales and research labs. Some folks are still working the land. Is there any teaching about farm life and agriculture?

You are right, of course. Plenty of people make a living by working the land and the percentage of those who do so in many nations remains quite high when compared to the United States. That is why, since the major documents of CST are often exercises of the universal magisterium of the church, one can find much attention paid to agriculture since it is the common labor of many in our world. John Paul II puts it simply; "The world of agriculture which provides society with the goods it needs for its daily sustenance, is of fundamental importance" (*Laborem Exercens,* #21).

Farming has its distinctive characteristics and the lifestyle of those who are farmers has its own rhythms, opportunities and troubles. It should also be noted that the experience of farming is different from one place to another. Without denying this, it is important to insist that much of what has been said already about human work applies to agriculture. "All that has been said thus far on the dignity of work, on the objective and subjective dimensions of human work, can be directly applied to the question of agricultural work and to the situation of the person who cultivates the earth by toiling in the fields" *(Ibid.).*

Over the years the annual conference of the U.N. Food and Agricultural Organization has been the occasion for Pius XII, John XXIII, Paul VI and John Paul II to speak directly to issues of farm life. In these addresses numerous topics have been touched upon, often focusing on the economic and social aspects of agricultural life. Another opportunity for developing CST on agriculture has been the frequent travels of John Paul where he regularly finds a locale from which to address gatherings of rural and farm workers.

Themes that regularly appear in CST when it treats agriculture are its link with development in poor countries; the need to respect nature through sustainable use of the environment; just treatment of farm workers, especially those who are migrants and guest workers; and, in those richer nations where agriculture is dominated by large corporations, the value of the family farm.

Six

International Life

74. In a number of your responses you have touched on matters that go beyond the nation-state. Are there any documents that focus specifically on the international context of social issues?

As you might imagine, treatment of war and peace requires moving beyond a domestic or national framework. Over the years, as the global dimensions of economic life have become more evident, CST has cast its economic teaching in an international context. Another factor pressing CST to become more international in scope is the emergence of a whole range of issues that are inherently transnational, for example, the environment, capital investment, human rights, migrants and refugees, the arms trade, the role of poor nations in the global economy.

Pius XII used his annual *urbi et orbi* (to the city and the world) Christmas radio addresses to discuss the structure of peace and international life that should be established at the cessation of World War II. John XXIII presented his ideas on international affairs in *Pacem in Terris,* and his earlier letter *Mater et Magistra* included attention to global economic issues.

Most notable, I think, is the 1967 letter *Populorum Progressio* of Paul VI. Scholars suggest that the reason for Paul's letter is his sensitivity to the plight of the poorer nations and his recognition that Vatican II was an event dominated largely by the pastoral agenda of Europe and the North American continents. Consequently, Paul wished to put the church squarely on the side of those who were calling for new efforts at development of poor nations.

In Paul's mind "the principal fact that we must all recognize is that the social question has become worldwide" (#3). Placing the social question in an international context, Paul opened up a new vista for CST. This approach was further considered at the 1971 synod with the statement *Justitia in Mundo* and Paul's letter *Octogesima Adveniens* commemorating *Rerum Novarum.* Twenty years after *Populorum Progressio,* John Paul II promulgated *Sollicitudo Rei Socialis,* which is his updating of, and expansion upon, the themes of Paul's letter.

In addition, I should mention that many episcopal conferences have written impressive documents on international matters. Most notable were the variety of major statements issued in the 1980s on nuclear deterrence, the arms race, war and peace.

75. If Jesus is our true peace and if we will only know that peace in our hearts, why should bishops or any of us focus on political ideas about peace rather than the spiritual?

It is important to make distinctions in our use of religious language and imagery. There is a perfectly valid sense in which Jesus is the living bread who alone satisfies our hunger, yet within the next few hours most of us will be eating something. To understand Jesus as living bread does not mean Christians can neglect the basic need for wholesome nutrition and hydration.

Something similar applies when we speak of Jesus as our true peace. There are many meanings to the term *peace*. As the U.S. bishops have written, "peace can refer to an individual's sense of well-being or security, or it can mean the cessation of armed hostility....For men and women of faith, peace will imply a right relationship with God, which entails forgiveness, reconciliation, and union. Finally, the scriptures point to the eschatological peace, a final, full realization of God's salvation..." (*The Challenge of Peace,* #27). We can see that peace is a word variously used.

Peace, in the eschatological sense, is a gift from God that cannot be attained through human effort. Peace, in the sense of a cessation of hostility, is a human possibility achievable in history. It is a real but pale expression of the future peace promised by God. Nonetheless, there are goals identified in CST that can promote this worldly peace which anticipates the true peace only God can create. These tasks are: psychological (changed attitudes), political (developing common security), economic (fair and just development) and military (arms control and nonprovocative strategies).

Without denying the sense in which Jesus is our true peace, CST seeks to articulate the appropriate values, norms and strategies that help to build the kind of peace that is not the fullness of peace but which is still an important accomplishment. Just as feeding a hungry nation is no mean achievement, yet it still falls short of the heavenly banquet, so, too, building a just and stable peace is an admirable goal even if it is not the fullness of the peace we seek.

76. What does CST mean by the just war tradition?

I want to make a distinction between the words *tradition* and *theory* in responding to your question. Within the same tradition you can have a variety of theories. Think of the Christian tradition; there are any number of theories, or we more commonly say theologies, within the tradition, yet they all are part of the Christian tradition. Paul, Augustine, Bonaventure, Aquinas, Luther and Calvin are just a few major theologians of the tradition. Despite their differences they all stand within the Christian tradition. So, too, with just war, there are any number of theories within the tradition. Some are complementary, others are in contradiction to each other, but they are all theories within the tradition. You may find one or another theory of just war unacceptable without rejecting the whole tradition.

The heart of the tradition is the belief that war is a rule-governed activity. War is part of the moral world, not apart from it. Unlike pacifists who cannot accept that war is a correct moral choice, or others whose zealotry leads them to think war is simply about winning at whatever price, the just war proponent argues that meaningful moral lines can be drawn in initiating wars and in waging them.

Properly understood, just war thinking is not pro-war or an advocacy of violence. "The Church's teaching on war and peace establishes a strong presumption against war which is binding on all; it then examines when this presumption may be overridden, precisely in the name of preserving the kind of peace which protects human dignity and human rights" (*Gaudium et Spes,* #70).

If one accepts just war thinking, three things must be remembered: (1) the burden of proof is on those who would override a moral duty not to kill or harm another; (2) to say that such a duty may be overridden in one case is not to override the duty in all cases; (3) the means of overriding should be as compatible as possible with a sense of regret for overriding the obligation not to kill.

77. What are the criteria that CST lists for a just war?

CST has developed its criteria in response to three questions: Why can force be used? When can force be used? How can force be used?

Answering the first question requires the articulation of what has come to be called the criterion of just cause. Various understandings of what counts as a just cause have been offered over the centuries. Modern Catholic teaching has pretty much restricted the use of violent force to resistance to another's aggression. Recently, there have been arguments to permit some cases of aid to innocents being abused by their government, what is called humanitarian intervention.

Making a case for a just cause is just the beginning of the process. I will follow the American bishops in explaining the additional criteria that address the questions when to go to war and how to wage war (*The Challenge of Peace*, #87–99).

• Competent authority: any decision to go to war must be made by the person or persons who are duly empowered to act on behalf of the common good.

• Comparative justice: this refers to the need to determine which side is sufficiently right in its complaint about the other side.

• Right intention: closely linked to just cause, this criterion calls for scrutiny of the motivation for war.

• Last resort: all reasonable peaceful alternatives must be tried before taking up arms.

• Probability of success: although often hard to assess, the idea is to avoid senseless or irrational use of force.

• Proportionality: this refers to some calculation of whether the good to be obtained by war outweighs the harm which will be caused.

• When the criteria for why and when are addressed it remains to assess the means. It is important to evaluate the methods employed by combatants. As frequently acknowledged, there are crimes in war even if war itself is not a crime.

• Discrimination: the most important distinction that must be made is between combatants and non-combatants.

• Proportionality: the assessment of good and evil should be applied not just to the overall war but to the particular tactics and weapons used in the fighting of the war.

• Clearly the just war tradition is meant to engage, not replace, our moral judgment. Essentially, the tradition is a set of questions and criteria to order our thinking logically, fairly and comprehensively when determining whether the presumption against violence holds.

78. A concern I have is how we can stand by and watch innocent people suffer at the hands of dictators who are little more than thugs. What does CST say about the possibility of humanitarian interventions?

CST's approach to humanitarian intervention is shaped by its understanding of political sovereignty, human rights, solidarity and international order.

In *Pacem in Terris,* John XXIII described the sovereignty of a state as restrained by forces that are both "higher" and "lower" than the state. The state has a legitimate role but it is bounded by the persons making up society and the role of states in the makeup of international society. Thus, "from below," the state must respect the human rights of individual human beings who have basic needs, essential freedoms and fundamental relationships. "From above" the state is limited by the duty to cooperate with other states and nongovernmental institutions in creating a global order that serves the international common good. State sovereignty, therefore, cannot be absolute but must be tempered by the rights of the human person and the goal of international community. Applied to humanitarian intervention, this suggests that state sovereignty must not be used to excuse grievous abuses of human rights.

When John Paul II discussed solidarity in *Sollicitudo Rei Socialis* he saw it as a virtue that allows people to "feel personally affected by the injustices and violations of human rights committed in distant countries" (#15). Looking at humanitarian intervention through the lens of solidarity means "states no longer have a 'right to indifference'" according to John Paul II. Instead, they have a duty to end injustice since "principles of the sovereignty of states and of non-interference in their internal affairs—which retain all their value—cannot constitute a screen behind which torture and murder may be carried out" (*Address to Diplomatic Corps Accredited to the Holy See, L'Osservatore Romano,* January 20, 1993).

In light of the above, there is a case to be made for humanitarian intervention as a possibility, even a duty within CST.

79. Frankly, I don't understand how we can talk about a just war. Maybe in the past this was possible, but today it simply is impossible to see the destruction caused by modern weapons and believe there is anything just about it. When will the church give up on the just war tradition and simply say, "war is wrong, period"?

You are certainly correct that modern warfare with its destructive power and its tendency to cause high ratios of civilian deaths to military combatants poses a challenge to the just war tradition. Even if war can be just in principle, many wonder whether a modern war can be just. I have no crystal ball but if a reversal of the church's acceptance of the just war tradition is forthcoming it will likely be incremental, not through a sudden pronouncement at the level of the universal magisterium.

Within the Catholic theological tradition the just war argument draws on several themes. In the area of eschatology, it is the tension of what has been called life during the in-between times, that is living in accord with the demands of God's reign while the fullness of that reign awaits the future. The mystery of human sin permeates our personal and social existence. We cannot ignore evil but should resist it even with means that are themselves tainted by sin's perduring effects. Catholic ecclesiology supports an understanding of the church that acknowledges some responsibility for a society's common good; the church should not withdraw from the sometimes messy affairs of temporal life.

Roman Catholic moral theology does not see physical life as an absolute good never to be sacrificed. While not to be taken without serious reason, human life is to be held in balance with competing goods and can be forsaken at times. CST laments the lack of an international authority that can regulate human affairs for the purpose of the common good. Given the structural void for resolving international disputes, the state has a right to defend itself against an aggressor.

Despite what has just been said, it is undoubtedly true that the horrible experience of war in the modern era is shaping CST. John Paul II has on numerous occasions presumed the validity of the just war idea, yet one would be hard-pressed to find a specific war about which he has not voiced doubts or outright opposition.

80. Don't you think we should talk less about just war and more about peace?

It is true, I admit, that we have spent more time on war-avoidance or war-regulation than we have on the positive task of building peace and articulating a theology of peace. That is changing.

In *Pacem in Terris,* John XXIII sketched a vision of peace including politics as service to the common good, the protection and promotion of human rights and new international structures to settle conflict nonviolently (#130–45). For John peace, as more than simply the absence of war, means humankind living in harmonious community and sharing the goods of life together.

Attaining this vision of peaceful existence through the practice of nonviolence has gotten renewed attention as a result of the collapse of the communist bloc with a minimum of violence. Commenting on those events, John Paul II has observed, "May people learn to fight for justice without violence, renouncing class struggle in their internal disputes and war in international ones" (*Centesimus Annus,* #23).

Other documents of CST address the nature and practices of peacemaking. Pius XII devoted many of his Christmas addresses to the topic of peace and the conditions for building a just and lasting peace after World War II. A constant theme of the papacy of Paul VI was that peace and justice are inextricably linked. It is impossible to have true peace without renewed dedication to the attainment of a more just, participatory, integral development within and between nations. Of late, John Paul has made the connection between peace and environmentalism. Peace is linked to new policies and programs that respect the natural environment

(*The Ecological Crisis: A Common Responsibility,* World Day of Peace Message, 1990).

It is fair to say that CST's development of a theology of peace is still a work in progress. The positive conception of peace endorsed by church teaching inevitably leads to a broad vision that embraces not only cessation of violence and nonviolent conflict resolution strategies but the securing of justice and the building of community wherein the unity of God's creation is incarnated.

81. Can you explain where pacifism fits into CST?

Among the most noteworthy developments in CST is the change from opposition to approval of pacifism. As recently as 1956 Pius XII maintained that a "Catholic citizen cannot invoke his own conscience in order to refuse to serve" in a war if the legitimate leaders of a nation declared war (*Christmas Radio Address,* 1956). This was not a novel position but one consistent with earlier papal teaching.

Just nine years later the bishops at Vatican II proclaimed: "We cannot fail to praise those who renounce the use of violence in the vindication of their rights and who resort to methods of defense which are otherwise available to weaker parties too, provided that this can be done without injury to the rights and duties of others or of the community itself" (*Gaudium et Spes,* #78).

The endorsement of pacifism is a qualified one, however. By that I do not mean that pacifism is halfheartedly embraced but that the pacifism which is supported by CST has a specific meaning. It is not sufficient simply for a person to oppose war in order to be a true pacifist. The objection to war must be based on moral grounds, not utility, opportunism, cowardice or inconvenience. Pacifism, as supported by CST, is the conviction that war is to be rejected because it is immoral.

Pacifism must also be situated within CST's commitment to justice. As the bishops at the council noted, a pacifist must not be indifferent to the "rights and duties of others or of the community itself." Human rights and the cause of justice must be defended at all times although not by all means as pacifists may eschew war.

A final qualification of pacifism in CST is that it is not a moral obligation but a moral option. What the bishops supported was the right of a person to refuse to participate in war on the basis of conscience. Pacifism was affirmed in deference to the dignity of the person's conscience, not because CST now renounced the just war tradition.

82. You said the bishops at Vatican II endorsed the right of Catholics to refuse to participate in war. Do you mean conscientious objection?

Yes, and this is one of the major developments in CST in our time. Once the church came to accept an individual's commitment to pacifism as a way of working for a just peace, it had to address the issue of what should be the public policy for such an approach. In keeping with their appreciation of the rights of conscience vis-à-vis the authority of the state (*Gaudium et Spes,* #16), the bishops at Vatican II saw that there had to be legal provision for pacifism lest individuals be coerced to act against their conscience or punished for following it. Thus, the church supported public policies that would allow a pacifist to have an alternative means of serving the common good and the cause of justice. As the bishops wrote: "It seems right that laws make humane provisions for the case of those who for reasons of conscience refuse to bear arms, provided, however, that they accept some other form of service to the human community" (#79).

There has also arisen the question of selective conscientious objection owing to the church's affirmation of the just war tradition in an age of total war and weapons of mass destruction. In the late 1960s, the bishops of the United States endorsed legal protection for those who refuse to serve in specific conflicts or in particular branches of the military that might require performing morally objectionable acts. Since then, the American bishops have reaffirmed on several occasions their support not only for conscientious objection but selective conscientious objection based on just war criteria.

The moral logic is clear: To reason within the just war tradition means some wars may be just but not all wars. However, as the bishops recognize, there are practical problems with codifying such a moral stance. "Selective conscientious objection poses complex, substantive and procedural problems, which must be worked out by moralists, lawyers and civil servants in a way that respects the rights of conscience without undermining the military's ability to defend the common good"

(USCC, "Declaration on Conscientious Objection and Selective Conscientious Objection," October 21, 1971, in *The Harvest of Justice Is Sown in Peace,* Part I, sec. c).

83. What does the church say about the arms race?

In *Pacem in Terris,* John XXIII looked with dismay upon the "enormous stocks of armaments that have been and still are being made in more economically developed countries" (#109). What is missing is the proper foundation for reversing the arms race. "[T]he fundamental principle on which our present peace depends must be replaced by another, which declares that the true and solid peace of nations consists not in equality of arms but in mutual trust alone" (#113).

This same chord is struck again at Vatican II where the bishops declared that "the arms race in which so many countries are engaged is not a safe way to preserve a steady peace. Nor is the so-called balance resulting from this race a sure and authentic peace" (*Gaudium et Spes,* #81). In the minds of the bishops the arms race is "an utterly treacherous trap for humanity and one which injures the poor to an intolerable degree" *(Ibid.).* Opposition to the arms race rests on three complaints.

First is the threat of nuclear war. Church leaders, both in the United States and abroad, are unconvinced that a balance of terror is a stable and a reasonable substitute for serious efforts at mutual reductions and disarmament.

Another criticism of the arms race is due to the tremendous growth in the damage capacity of nonnuclear, conventional weapons. While the world has been spared a nuclear war, there have been numerous wars that have been highly destructive. Not only sophisticated air attacks but even modern ground wars have wreaked great destruction.

Finally, CST has linked opposition to the arms race to its concern for economic development among poor populations. Paul VI and John Paul II have been especially direct in their calls for a reallocation of resources—economic, technological, human—away from the arms race and toward development.

For these three reasons the evaluation of the arms race as found in CST is harsh. It is no exaggeration to say that CST views the arms race as one of the great evils of the modern era.

84. Speaking of great evils, I heard someone say the Catholic Church teaches that the gap between rich and poor nations is the great evil of our time. Is that true?

The growing gap between rich and poor has been an urgent concern for some time. In 1961 the issue grabbed John XXIII's attention: "Perhaps the most pressing question of our day concerns the relationship between economically advanced commonwealths and those that are in process of development" (*Mater et Magistra,* #157).

At Vatican II, overcoming the division between rich and poor was given a theological reading when the bishops declared that "the promotion of human unity belongs to the innermost nature of the Church" and that the church must function as "a sacramental sign and an instrument of intimate unity with God, and of the unity of all humankind" (*Gaudium et Spes,* #42). CST does not demand a strict equality in all matters between people. However, when the gaps between groups become so great that the church's claims of unity start to ring hollow a theological crisis emerges.

Paul VI expressed dismay that the world economy left unreformed works "to widen the differences in the world's levels of life, not to diminish them" (*Populorum Progressio,* #8). In the face of this reality Paul offered hope that "a true communion of all nations be achieved" (#43), and he pointed out that this should be a "concern especially of better-off nations" (#44).

Using terminology common by the decade of the 1980s, John Paul II writes: "We can understand the current usage which speaks of different worlds within our one world: the First World, the Second World, the Third World, and, at times the Fourth World" (*Sollicitudo Rei Socialis,* #14). Such language is significant since it reflects "a widespread sense that the unity of the world, that is, the unity of the human race, is seriously compromised" *(Ibid.).*

Clearly, the situation of great poverty for most amidst great wealth for a minority is a moral and a religious concern from the perspective of Catholicism. The church has as its vocation to be a sacrament of unity witnessing to God's purposes; working to overcome the harsh divisions within the created order is intimately linked to that religious vocation (*Sollicitudo Rei Socialis,* #31).

85. What is the remedy for the gap between rich and poor?

In a word *development,* but this term requires explanation since one finds in CST an evolution in its usage. One might say that there has been development in the church's teaching on development!

Although John XIII called in 1961 for increased financial aid and emergency assistance to poor nations where this was needed, he realized the underlying causes of the plight of the world's poor had to be addressed in a new way. The year he wrote *Mater et Magistra* was also the beginning of the U.N. First Development Decade. There was optimism that something akin to the Marshall Plan, which helped rebuild postwar Europe, might happen in Africa, Asia and Latin America.

John laid out three basic norms for development: (a) the internal affairs of poor nations should be reformed to ensure efficiency and fairness (#167–68); (b) all efforts should be made to avoid a cultural imperialism by which economically advanced nations disrupt the cultural systems of aid recipients (#169–71); and (c) new developments in international economic life should not lead to an economic colonialism that replaces the older political colonialism experienced by a number of the poor nations (#172).

Paul VI articulated a threefold obligation of the richer nations: the duty of human solidarity, the duty of social justice and the duty of universal charity (*Populorum Progressio,* #44). The first duty pointed out the need for generous and wisely planned aid to poorer nations (#45–55). The second duty of social justice required nations to address in a systematic manner the necessary reform of the economic framework governing international trade (#56–65). Finally, Paul wrote of the duty of charity that called for sensitivity to cultural differences and respect for local customs, as well as hospitality toward immigrants and a spirit of mutual collaboration between rich and poor (#66–75).

Taken together, these guidelines articulate the elements of what makes for just development. Important as it is, however, "just" was but the first modifier to precede the noun *development* in CST. The next expression was *integral development.*

86. What is "integral development"?

Paul VI was troubled by the lack of progress in addressing development during the 1960s. He wanted to clarify the Catholic perspective on the goal of development since in his mind some approaches to the question were reductionistic, focused only on increasing the gross national product of a nation or the average per capita income of a person.

Paul emphasized that "development cannot be limited to mere economic growth. In order to be authentic, it must be complete: integral, that is, it has to promote the good of every person and the whole person" (*Populorum Progressio,* #14). The pope was clear that "increased possession is not the ultimate goal of nations nor of individuals. All growth is ambivalent." The ambivalence owes to the fact that economic well-being is essential, but it is also a trap hindering true development if the person makes economic goods the supreme good (#19).

For Paul there are stages that lead to integral development. "The passage from misery toward the possession of necessities, victory over social scourges, the growth of knowledge, the acquisition of culture" are all important, indeed essential, first steps. Also needed are "increased esteem for the dignity of the others, the turning toward the spirit of poverty, cooperation for the common good, the will and desire for peace." Even more humanizing are "the acknowledgment by the person of supreme values, and of God their source and their finality." Finally, human development climaxes with "faith, a gift of God accepted by the good will of the individual, and unity in the charity of Christ" which permits us to share in the very life of God (#21).

John Paul II has also picked up on the idea that development has a richer meaning than the single goal of economic improvement. For John Paul, development is not the same as the myth of progress in the West nor can it be confused with consumerism. Development has an economic dimension but is not solely economic (*Sollicitudo Rei Socialis,* #28). Genuine development is integral; it has moral and spiritual dimensions as well as political, cultural and economic (#27–34).

87. So is just and integral development the basic message of CST on this topic?

Writing four years after Paul's encyclical the bishops assembled at the 1971 synod spoke about "liberation through development" (*Justitia in Mundo,* ch. 1). By this time the Latin American bishops had met in Medellin, Colombia. That conference was a turning point for the church in

Latin America for it was there that the bishops of that region hammered out a pastoral plan for implementing the renewal called for at Vatican II.

By using the expression "liberation through development" the bishops were calling for processes of development that were not controlled by economic elites living in either the richer or poorer nations. There was, in the viewpoint of the bishops, a "real danger that the conditions of life created by colonial domination may evolve into a new form of colonialism" *(Ibid.)* In short, economic colonialism might happen if development was simply a "top down" process.

The word *liberation* was intended to signal that any appropriate development strategy had to engage the grass roots. "By taking their future into their own hands through a determined will for progress, the developing peoples—even if they do not achieve the final goal—will authentically manifest their own personalization" *(Ibid.).* Evident here is the realization that development is not simply a goal but a process and that certain qualities should characterize the process leading to economic advancement. For the bishops at the synod, development is "composed both of economic growth and participation," this latter term being used to suggest theories of development that are inclusive of and directed, at least in part, by the poor themselves *(Ibid.).* So, in addition to just and integral, the modifier *participatory* became part of CST's approach to development.

88. Is any other dimension of development needed to grasp the approach of CST?

Another aspect of development began to grab the attention of church leaders by 1971. At the beginning of the first chapter of the synod statement, there is the comment that among the changes in our world is the dawning awareness that material "resources, as well as the precious treasures of air and water—without which there cannot be life—and the small delicate biosphere of the whole complex of all life on earth, are not infinite, but on the contrary must be saved and preserved..." (*Justitia in Mundo,* chapter 1).

A few lines later the bishops linked their emerging ecological consciousness with the development issue: "Such is the demand for resources and energy by the richer nations, whether capitalist or socialist, and such are the effects of dumping by them in the atmosphere and the sea that irreparable damage would be done to the essential elements of life on earth, such as air and water, if their high rates of consumption and pollution, which are constantly on the increase, were extended to the whole of humankind" *(Ibid.)*.

By 1987 the issues surrounding care of the environment had become prominent in the minds of many authors who wrote about development, among them John Paul II. For him a proper approach to development cannot "exclude respect *for the beings which constitute* the natural world *(Sollicitudo Rei Socialis,* #34, emphasis in document). Thus, "a true concept of development cannot ignore the use of the elements of nature, the renewability of resources and the consequences of haphazard industrialization" *(Ibid.)*. As a result, we can add a fourth modifier before the word development, namely, *sustainable.*

Just development means concern for establishing fairness among the nations of the world. Integral development means achieving the proper balance between material goods and other aspects of human well-being. Participatory development requires that poor people and nations be considered agents capable of self-determination and of advancing their own development. Sustainable development calls attention to fairness between one generation and the next and within generations on the use of the resources given by God to all.

89. One issue that received a lot of attention during the Holy Year 2000 is the jubilee theme of debt forgiveness. Does CST address the issue of international debt?

This specific issue should be seen as a piece of the larger topic of development. In *Populorum Progressio* Paul VI hoped for a situation where "developing countries will thus no longer risk being overwhelmed by debts whose repayment swallows up the greater part of their gains" (#54).

This call for an approach that would be more helpful to the poor nations of the world led the Pontifical Commission on Justice and Peace to issue *Ethical Dimensions of the International Debt* in 1986. This document put the church squarely on record as being in favor of restructuring loan arrangements and forgiving debt in more extreme cases. Since then, John Paul II has described the international debt crisis as a sign of the interdependence of nations and as a reality that has a *"close connection"* with the "development of peoples" (*Sollicitudo Rei Socialis,* #19, emphasis in text).

For John Paul, "the instrument chosen to make a contribution to development has turned into a counterproductive mechanism." What has happened is that the debt service has become "a *brake* upon development" and "even *aggravated underdevelopment*" (*Ibid.,* emphasis in text). At this point, the ethical question of development's purpose must be factored into any reckoning of what poor nations owe to creditors.

And so in preparation for the jubilee year 2000 the U.S. bishops proposed seven guidelines for debt relief: (1) Include all the poor nations in any plan, not just a select few. (2) Make sure that whatever resources are freed through debt relief are used to reduce poverty. (3) Ensure that the people of poor nations are able to influence the decision-making process regarding debt alleviation. (4) Require that economic reform in poor nations attend to the needs of the worst off. (5) Implement safeguards so that corruption and waste do not prevent debt relief from helping those who most need it. (6) Provide adequate funding with fair cost-sharing among creditors. (7) Use debt forgiveness as a piece of a larger effort to achieve sustainable development for poor nations (*A Jubilee Call for Debt Forgiveness,* Sec. III).

90. A key role in debt relief and numerous other questions in international life is played by global institutions such as the World Bank, the International Monetary Fund (I.M.F.) and, of course, the United Nations. What has CST to say about these organizations?

When the church looks at the world situation, it sees what has been termed a "structural flaw" in the international order. In national life, there is the institution of the state that is charged with the responsibility to promote the common good. But there is no comparable institution to perform this role for the global common good.

Efforts to foster cooperation among states and to develop institutions, policies and regulations that are international in scope are ordinarily viewed favorably by the church. Indeed, the most common lament by the papacy is that international institutions are too weak or underutilized. For example, Pius XII was disappointed by the inability of the United Nations to surmount the ideological obstacles of the cold war and become a genuine alternative forum for settling disputes without recourse to war.

This papal disappointment did not lead to abandonment of the United Nations, however, since the Vatican is quite supportive of the organization. Paul VI and John Paul II have both spoken before the U.N. General Assembly, and the Holy See has an official diplomatic presence within the U.N. structure.

Although one can find areas of disagreement (e.g., theories of development) and specific criticisms (e.g., criteria for loans) of international economic institutions such as the I.M.F. there is agreement with the general principle of such organizations in CST. One can find a sort of summary of John Paul's opinion in his 1987 encyclical. "The existing institutions and organizations have worked well for the benefit of peoples. Nevertheless, humanity today is in a new and more difficult phase of its genuine development. It needs a *greater degree of international ordering,* at the service of societies, economies and cultures of the whole world" (*Sollicitudo Rei Socialis,* #43, emphasis in document).

In the church's teaching on interdependence, solidarity and the common good there is a foundation for approval of international organizations if they are dedicated to the promotion of the global common good and at the service of human dignity and human rights.

91. Obviously, a major global issue today is the health and integrity of our environment. What does CST say about the concerns of the ecological movement?

As noted earlier (Q. 88) there was in 1971 at the synod a concern expressed about the environment in the context of discussions of development. Months earlier Paul VI had made reference to the "ill-considered exploitation of nature" that was leading to "an environment for tomorrow which may well be intolerable" (*Octogesima Adveniens,* #21).

It is during the papacy of John Paul II, however, that attention to the natural environment has increased in CST. The pope named a growing awareness for "the need to respect the integrity and the cycles of nature" as one of the positive signs of the times (*Sollicitudo Rei Socialis,* #26). Four years later, he suggested that "at the root of the senseless destruction of the natural environment lies an anthropological error," which is that people think they "can make arbitrary use of the earth...as though it did not have its own requisites and a prior God-given purpose" (*Centesimus Annus,* #37).

More significant than these comments was John Paul's World Day of Peace Message in 1990 where he developed an argument for the moral nature of the ecological crisis and pointed out the common responsibility that we all have for preserving the integrity of creation *(The Ecological Crisis: A Common Responsibility).* Before and since this papal statement a variety of episcopal conferences have issued pastoral statements or letters that have taken up the topic of the environment from their local perspective.

A survey of these documents suggests that CST offers a number of principles that can frame discussion of the environment: (a) the goods of the earth belong to all; (b) there is a human right to a safe environment; (c) nature's diversity is a reflection of God's grandeur; (d) awareness of the beauty of the created order is a classic path to contemplation of God's beauty and love; (e) the right of the poor to true development must not be sacrificed in the correction of ecological abuses; and (f) the wide scope of environmental issues requires a new global solidarity.

SEVEN

SPECIFIC CONCERNS

92. What does CST have to say about women in society?

In accord with the prevailing cultural and social views of women at the time, Leo XIII and Pius XI often defended the dignity of women by presuming that dignity meant some social roles and tasks were against women's nature: "Women, again, are not suited to certain trades, for a woman is by nature fitted for home work, and it is that which is best adapted at once to preserve her modesty, and to promote the good bringing up of children and the well-being of the family" (*Rerum Novarum*, #33).

John XXIII noted approvingly the change in social roles for women as a sign of the times and explicitly asserted that family life is to be arranged with "equal rights and duties for man and woman" (*Pacem in Terris*, #15). Vatican II proclaimed "everyone should acknowledge and favor the proper and necessary participation of women in cultural life" (*Gaudium et Spes*, #60). Paul VI strongly supported these claims but did have concerns about what he judged to be excesses in some feminist claims about women's role in society.

John Paul II affirms the equality of the sexes although there is a tendency to see a predetermined set of complementary roles for women and men. He returns to the earlier language of a family wage, that is a salary given to the man "sufficient for the needs of the family without the spouse having to take up gainful employment outside the home" (*Laborem Exercens*, #19). Still, when employed, a woman has the same rights as a man and all discrimination based on sex should be removed from the work place.

Contemporary CST sees women as being equal in dignity and in rights to men. Discrimination in the work place, in cultural life, in government is unacceptable. In social reform women are encouraged to bring gospel values into public life. It must be said, however, that the functions of parenting and homemaking are still closely attached to women in a way that is not the case when papal teaching speaks of men and their social tasks.

93. Does CST say anything about racism and race relations?

Generally racism is treated under the broader topic of discrimination; "with respect to the fundamental rights of the person, every type of discrimination, whether social or cultural, whether based on sex, race, color, social condition, language or religion, is to be overcome and eradicated as contrary to God's intent" (*Gaudium et Spes,* #29).

A statement on race was being prepared during the end of Pius XI's pontificate. This so-called lost encyclical was never completed after his death. On various occasions popes have spoken against racism, but it was not until 1988 that a specific document on racism was issued by the Pontifical Commission on Justice and Peace: *The Church and Racism: Towards a More Fraternal Society.* The document traces racism throughout history and identifies forms of racism today. It then offers a theological reflection defending the dignity of each human person and the essential unity of the human race. The concluding section offers suggested remedies for the evil of racism.

In the universal church the discussion on race has a different context than here in the United States. Treatment of native peoples in the colonies of the New World, discrimination against and persecution of Jews in Europe, the rise of the slave trade from Africa—these are all cases that confronted the church in its history and shape its understanding of racism.

With regard to the U.S. context, the most important episcopal statements began with *Brothers and Sisters to Us,* a pastoral letter on racism issued in 1979. This was followed by a letter from all the black bishops, *What We Have Seen and Heard,* issued five years later. In the first document racism was explicitly identified as a sin and denounced. There was also a call to combat the racism that is more subtle than outright discrimination in public policy, namely the kind expressed in personal attitudes, social isolation, economic marginalization. The letter by the black bishops looked at the gifts and charisms within their community that were being untapped and which might enrich the church if more successful evangelization occurred.

94. A big issue in my region of the nation is immigration. What, if anything, does CST have to say about immigration?

CST distinguishes between refugees and migrants. The latter are people who pick up and move to another locale voluntarily or involuntarily. The words emigrant and immigrant simply designate migrants from the vantage point of the place of departure or arrival. Refugees are that subgroup of migrants who flee involuntarily because their homeland is no longer hospitable. War, terrorism and natural disasters are common causes of refugeeism.

CST expresses a strong concern for the basic rights of refugees. John XXIII expressed the conviction central to the church's position: "Refugees are persons and all their rights as persons must be recognized. Refugees cannot lose their rights simply because they are deprived of citizenship in their own states" (*Pacem in Terris,* #105). Refugees have a strong right to asylum in CST: "Any person in danger who appears at a frontier has a right to protection." This is not a concession on the part of the host nation for the refugee "is not an object of assistance, but rather a subject of rights and duties" (*Refugees: A Challenge to Solidarity,* #4). Asylum is a human right not to be compromised.

When examining voluntary migration CST acknowledges a human right to emigrate but distinguishes it from the right to immigrate. The fact that a person is a member of a state does not cancel the reality of being part of the human family and it is on this basis that the right to emigrate is founded. Immigration should be permitted but it can be regulated. While generally CST presumes the immigrant is to be accepted, it is possible that a state may have to regulate immigration in order to meet its obligations to those already living within its borders.

An additional concern of the church is the treatment of migrants who come to another country to find a job. Whether permanent or seasonal, such workers are to be treated fairly. As John Paul II wrote: "Emigration in search of work must in no way become an opportunity for financial or social exploitation" (*Laborem Exercens,* #23).

95. It seems as if the death penalty has become a concern in this country and I know that John Paul II opposes it. What does CST say about capital punishment?

CST has long recognized the right of the state to use deadly force to defend the common good of society. The argument flows from Catholic political theory and the understanding of the state as the agent that secures public order. This entails certain duties and responsibilities among which are the duties to protect the members of society and to safeguard public morality. Both soldiers and police officers are examples of people who may, under certain conditions, kill as authorized agents of the state. Capital punishment understood as state imposed execution is but an illustration of the overarching duty of the state to protect the common good of a society.

Traditionally, we have said punishment should protect society (public safety and deterrence), reform the criminal and make retribution. How does this apply to capital punishment? Public safety is attainable in other ways since the person is now in custody. The death penalty's deterrent effect is a much contested issue. Execution makes reform of a criminal impossible. The remaining rationale is retribution and here the consensus is not as strong as it once was. In the minds of many, other penalties that serve all the objectives of punishment are thereby preferable to capital punishment.

Recent documents of CST reflect this growing caution about the death penalty. Present teaching can be summarized: (1) the state has the right to kill; (2) the decision to act on that right must be evaluated with attention to the context in which the right is to be exercised; (3) while the church does not say there is never a legitimate exercise of the state's right, it does suggest that in the present circumstances of American society it is unwise and unjustified to put criminals to death. This is the position espoused by John Paul II and included in the revised *Catechism of the Catholic Church,* where the principle of the state's right is acknowledged but it is then suggested that the cases in which the execution of the offender is an absolute necessity "are very rare, if not practically nonexistent" (John Paul II, *Evangelium Vitae,* #56).

96. In all your comments, I get no sense that CST has an ecumenical aspect. Does ecumenism figure in the tradition of CST?

It should not surprise us that the area of ecumenism in social teaching closely mirrors the attitude toward ecumenism in other areas of church teaching. So at a time when ecumenical cooperation was viewed with great reservation, even alarm, one finds in Leo XIII a desire to have labor organizations that are explicitly Catholic in membership, format and goals. Nor should it surprise us that it is with John XXIII we see a change in attitude. He was the first pope to address an encyclical "to all people of good will" when he issued *Pacem in Terris.* Toward the end of that letter he noted: "The putting of these [social] principles into effect frequently involves extensive cooperation between Catholics and those Christians who are separated from this Apostolic See. It even involves the cooperation of Catholics with people who may not be Christian but who nevertheless are reasonable and possess natural moral integrity....[Catholics] should show themselves animated by a spirit of understanding and unselfishness, ready to cooperate loyally in achieving objects which are good in themselves or conducive to good" (#157).

Openness to ecumenical cooperation has continued since then. The bishops at the 1971 synod wrote: "We very highly commend cooperation with our separated Christian brethren for the promotion of justice in the world, for bringing about development of people and for establishing peace" (*Justitia in Mundo,* ch. 3). John Paul II has strongly endorsed this attitude. Speaking of working for the development of peoples, he announced: "It obliges the Catholic Church and the other churches and ecclesial communities, with which we are completely willing to collaborate in this field. In this sense, just as we Catholics invite our Christian brethren to share in our initiatives, so too we declare that we are ready to collaborate in theirs, and we welcome the invitations presented to us" (*Sollicitudo Rei Socialis,* #32).

Undoubtedly, the experience of Catholics working at the grass roots for social change is that ecumenical and interreligious cooperation is a common and valued aspect of their labor.

97. I don't mean this in a mean-spirited way, but can you say that CST made any difference in the real world of American politics, economics and culture?

It would be a mistaken expectation that a politician would announce: "I am doing this because of what John XXIII said in *Pacem in Terris*." That does not mean CST has had no impact in this country. It has, and we might understand it as both direct and indirect.

The direct impact is evident in the numerous groups and individuals who have been motivated and guided by the teaching. Abundant organizations were formed under the rubric of Catholic Action in the 1930s and afterward that engaged thousands of people in consciously translating CST into public action. Many cities witnessed the phenomenon of the labor priest movement, and programs on labor rights and CST were once common. Lay groups in the United States such as the Catholic Worker and the Central Verein as well as church-based community organizations have contributed much to popular movements for social reform. Today, Catholic Charities USA, the Campaign for Human Development, Catholic Relief Services and the Catholic Health Association are organizations that espouse CST in the way they deliver social services and advocate for public policy. These and so many more examples could be cited to show that CST directly influenced the motivation and organization of Catholics to become involved in social change.

Indirectly, the impact is harder to calculate but it is there. All societies operate with a certain amount of "conventional wisdom," a taken-for-granted world of assumptions and ideas. Public policies and economic activity within the conventional wisdom are acceptable while those outside conventional wisdom do not get taken seriously. Important in the life of any group is who sets the boundaries of the conventional wisdom and what the boundaries are. Part of what CST has helped to do is make topics such as concern for the poor, the rights of workers and nuclear arms reductions part of the conventional wisdom of U.S. society. The ideals and principles of CST have helped to shape the political and economic thinking of U.S. citizens even among those people who would not associate with the Catholic Church on any other level.

98. Since my primary experience of the church is what happens in my parish, what can we do at the parish level to advance CST?

An excellent statement by the U.S. bishops provides insights for this concern. *Communities of Salt and Light: Reflections on the Social Mission of the Parish* explores how CST can influence just about every aspect of parish life—liturgy, preaching, adult faith formation, religious education for youth, finance and budgeting, volunteerism, lay ministry. The key concern is that parish-based social ministry not be seen as a specialized topic for a segment of the parish. Rather, the social mission of the church should be integrated into the entire range of parish life.

For the sake of directing that effort, it is often wise to develop a parish social ministry committee that sets as its task the integration of the social mission with the worship, formation and action of the parish community. There are any number of helpful guides and resources for such committees. One resource is the manual published to accompany *Communities of Salt and Light;* it contains many more suggestions than can be mentioned here.

When thinking about parish social ministry, two guiding principles I have long espoused are the 90–90 rule and the test for a good parish. The 90–90 rule is simply that for 90 percent of active Catholics the local parish is their only experience of church and for 90 percent of that group the weekend liturgy is their major experience of parish. Any agenda for parish action must absorb the implications of that rule.

My second principle is what constitutes the test of a good parish. I believe the common way of thinking must be reversed. For too many a parish is judged by how well it serves me and my family. The real test ought to be how well does the parish inspire, empower and sustain me and my family to serve others. Examining liturgy, preaching, education, parish staffing, budgeting, programming and organizations from that perspective can provide interesting results to advance CST in creative and innovative ways.

99. Is there much attention given to spirituality in CST?

There is certainly an assumption about the importance of a spirituality for justice and peace in CST. At Vatican II the bishops understood CST to be a response to "the impulses of the Spirit"; they wrote: "The

People of God believes that it is led by the Spirit of the Lord who fills the earth" (*Gaudium et Spes,* #11). One can understand the entire enterprise of developing a tradition of social teaching, therefore, as a process of faith-filled discernment, a reading of the signs of the times in a mode of prayerful contemplation. Yet there is not a great deal of explicit exposition regarding this spirituality to be found in most of the documents.

Certainly many biblical themes inform the vision of CST, and appeals are made to both the baptismal identity and eucharistic experience of the community in the documents. In the 1971 synod statement there is awareness of the educational role of the liturgy. As a thanksgiving to God in Christ, it has a communitarian form that holds up before our eyes the reality of our brother and sisterhood. "The liturgy of the word, catechesis, and the celebration of the sacraments have the power to help us discover the teaching of the prophets, the Lord, and the apostles on the subject of justice. The preparation for baptism is the beginning of the formation of the Christian conscience. The practice of penance should emphasize the social dimension of sin and of the sacrament. Finally, the Eucharist forms the community and places it at the service of humankind" (*Justitia in Mundo,* ch. 3).

One of the notable features of two pastoral letters of the U.S. bishops is that they have offered outlines of a spirituality for peacemaking (*The Challenge of Peace,* #290–300) and economic justice (*Economic Justice for All,* #327–36). Much more can be said, but there is a framework for a spirituality that sustains CST in those paragraphs.

100. I'd like to put you on the spot for two questions. First, up until now you have done your best to put a good face on CST. What criticisms of CST do you think are legitimate?

I am unable to list all the criticisms but I will give you four charges, in no particular order, that strike me as being on target.

Recall when I discussed the image of women I mentioned that one can find in many of the documents of CST the belief that there are some "natural" roles for women as mothers and full-time homemakers. This is a good example of a temptation to which CST sometimes falls prey, namely, to treat existing social arrangements as reflective of natural law or divine will rather than historically conditioned human decisions. The error is to "canonize" a given social institution or practice and lose sight of how all existing arrangements fall short of God's future.

A second difficulty for CST is coming to terms with the reality of conflict. The bias of communitarianism is so strong in CST that there is a reluctance to acknowledge the role of anything other than harmonious cooperation as a solution to social ills. Without endorsing a Marxist class conflict model of social change or equating conflict with violence, we need to be able to see the creative role that conflict can play in bringing about change. Only appealing to groups to overcome self-interest is not necessarily the best approach to managing conflict.

A third plausible criticism of CST is that the focus on the norms governing just distribution of goods has meant that the conditions that secure adequate production of goods are left inadequately examined. Because the lens used by CST to view economic issues has had workers at the center, there has not always been an understanding of the role of investors, managers and other agents in economic life.

A fourth criticism that must be taken seriously is the process of formulating the teaching. Too often it has been a process with little input from the wider church and little dialogue outside a small circle of often unnamed ghost writers. One can also ask if long encyclical letters are the best way to promulgate CST.

You said you had two questions.

101. My final question also asks you to take a risk. Can you predict the future of CST?

Well, I am not a soothsayer but it is safe to say that CST will continue to develop, sometimes in predictable ways. Clearly, the whole topic of globalization and related sub-issues will continue to grow in importance and my guess is that the church will have to give it increased attention.

We have seen the contribution that John Paul II has made to the tradition, due in part to his experience as a man of Polish heritage. I suspect if someday we have a pope from a non-European nation he will bring new perspectives and concerns to CST.

As the church becomes more and more sensitive to diversity, there will be a larger role for the local churches to play in formulating CST. Certainly this will involve episcopal conferences and they may, in turn, adopt methods of teaching that call for greater involvement by scholars, ordinary pastoral ministers and members of the faith community in formulating the teaching.

I would hazard a guess as well that certain topics that have been part of the tradition will be recast and examined with fresh eyes as the dynamics of change continue in our world. I am thinking here of the environment, the role of women, nonviolent alternatives to war, the use of technology and the communications revolution and, finally, violent behavior outside of war. These topics are simply my sense of the future agenda for CST, but the important thing for the life of the church is not that CST respond to some predetermined agenda. Rather, the hope is that we as a church continue to read the signs of the times in the light of the gospel and articulate to the best of our ability what faith says to the work of building a just, peaceful and sustainable world.

BIBLIOGRAPHY

Here is some additional reading that should be helpful to those seeking more information about Catholic social teaching. Not included is the literature cited in the text.

Bokenkotter, Thomas. *Church and Revolution: Catholics in the Struggle for Democracy and Social Justice* **(New York: Image Books, 1998)**
Through a series of historical vignettes of key individuals the author recounts much of the story of CST. Not intended as a synthesis or analysis of the documents of CST, it is a collection of telling portraits of people who have embodied the teaching. For serious adult readers.

Dorr, Donal. *Option for the Poor: A Hundred Years of Catholic Social Teaching* **(Maryknoll, N.Y.: Orbis Books, 1992)**
Although not comprehensive in its coverage of the tradition, this is a well-done historical account and analysis of modern CST. While not difficult to read, it does go into more detail than a casual reader might want.

Dwyer, Judith, ed. *The New Dictionary of Catholic Social Thought* **(Collegeville, Minn.: The Liturgical Press, 1994)**
Not a dictionary in the ordinary sense. Written by a number of scholars, it is more like an encyclopedia with articles arranged alphabetically that cover just about all the key figures, documents and ideas of CST. Scholarly, but still accessible to educated adults.

Himes, Michael. *Doing the Truth in Love: Conversations about God, Relationships and Service* **(New York: Paulist Press, 1995)**
    A collection of talks given to college students that make the connection between faith and social commitment. Provides a fine foundation for a spirituality of social justice. With many examples and stories, it is accessible to any adult.

Himes, Michael and Kenneth Himes. *Fullness of Faith: The Public Significance of Theology* **(New York: Paulist Press, 1993)**
    After an opening chapter that explains the discussion among scholars on what is often called "public theology," there are six chapters that demonstrate public theology: how basic symbols of our faith have implications not only for personal life but for social existence. For educated adults with an interest in theology.

Kammer, Fred. *Doing Faithjustice: An Introduction to Catholic Social Thought* **(New York: Paulist Press, 1991)**
    After two nicely done chapters on the biblical foundations, the third provides a brief historical summary followed by a schematic outline of each of the major documents of CST. The final chapters are reflections on what a commitment to the poor entails, how to act with justice as well as charity and guidance for implementing CST at the local level. Written for general audience.

Land, Philip. *Catholic Social Teaching: As I Have Lived, Loathed and Loved It* **(Chicago: Loyola University Press, 1994)**
    An autobiographical account of a Jesuit scholar's involvement in the promotion and formulation of CST. It is an intellectual history not only of CST but also the author's personal journey. Presumes more than basic knowledge of the tradition.

Massaro, Thomas. *Living Justice: Catholic Social Teaching in Action* **(Franklin, Wis.: Sheed and Ward, 2000)**
    An easy-to-read introduction to CST that is less concerned with the history and details of the documents and more with reflecting upon

how to enact the lessons of the teaching. A good companion to an adult discussion group on how to respond to the message of CST.

Mich, Marvin. *Catholic Social Teaching and Movements* (Mystic, Conn.: Twenty-Third Publications, 1998)
A fine telling of the story of CST; not only the key documents but also many of the grass-roots movements inspired by the tradition are covered. Can be read by those interested in the history at a popular level.

O'Brien, David and Thomas Shannon, eds. *Catholic Social Thought: The Documentary Heritage* (Maryknoll, N.Y.: Orbis Books, 1995)
One of the best collections of the documents of CST, it includes almost all of the documents I have cited in this book. Short introductions accompany each text. Although not light reading, these are the primary texts that give expression to the social mission of the church.

Other Books in the Series

RESPONSES TO 101 QUESTIONS ON THE BIBLE
by Raymond E. Brown, S.S.

RESPONSES TO 101 QUESTIONS ON THE DEAD SEA SCROLLS
by Joseph A. Fitzmyer, S.J.

RESPONSES TO 101 QUESTIONS ABOUT JESUS
by Michael L. Cook, S.J.

RESPONSES TO 101 QUESTIONS ABOUT FEMINISM
by Denise Lardner Carmody

RESPONSES TO 101 QUESTIONS ON THE PSALMS
AND OTHER WRITINGS
by Roland E. Murphy, O. Carm.

RESPONSES TO 101 QUESTIONS ON THE CHURCH
by Richard P. McBrien

RESPONSES TO 101 QUESTIONS ON THE BIBLICAL TORAH
by Roland E. Murphy, O. Carm.

RESPONSES TO 101 QUESTIONS ON BUSINESS ETHICS
by George Devine

RESPONSES TO 101 QUESTIONS ON DEATH AND
ETERNAL LIFE
by Peter C. Phan

RESPONSES TO 101 QUESTIONS ON ISLAM
by John Renard

RESPONSES TO 101 QUESTIONS ON HINDUISM
by John Renard

RESPONSES TO 101 QUESTIONS ON BUDDHISM
by John Renard

RESPONSES TO 101 QUESTIONS ON THE MASS
by Kevin W. Irwin

RESPONSES TO 101 QUESTIONS ON GOD AND EVOLUTION
by John F. Haught